BRISTOL 650

Essays on the Future of Bristol

Edited by Amy O'Beirne and Andrew Kelly

Bristol Books CIC, The Courtyard, Wraxall,
Wraxall Hill, Bristol, BS48 1NA
www.bristolbooks.org

Bristol 650: Essays on the Future of Bristol
Edited by Amy O'Beirne and Andrew Kelly

Published by Bristol Books 2023

ISBN: 9781909446373

Design: Joe Burt
Cover image: Till Lukat

Printed by Short Run Press, Exeter. Printed on paper from a sustainable source.

A CIP record of this book is available from the British Library

 This publication is made possible with support from The
National Lottery Heritage Fund and National Lottery players.

Bristol 650

Essays on the Future of Bristol

Introduction

1. Bristol to 2023

2. City Visions

3. Social Justice and Bristol

Everything Comes from Somewhere

Kat Lyons, City Poet 2022-2024

Everything comes from somewhere. Someone dreamed
a bridge across a gorge, set the first stone,
stepped out in 1864
onto what had once been empty air.

When evening stretches long as a lazy cat,
Bristol grows restless,
wanders through its library of centuries. Calls you to join it
shuffling through sheaves of years.

Cross the road and slip
into its scrapbook, flick through
anniversaries enshrined in architecture, blue plaques,
opened doors, emptied plinths.

Untie the ribbon on the charter, 650 years unroll. Parchment holds
a painted king, a gold-leaf crown. A royal seal
stamps a border, redraws a county. Snips a city out
and sends it off to seek its fortune on its own.

Bristol grows in concentric rings. Industry expands,
seeds quarries in the Kings Wood, forests of houses
in the Fish Ponds. Villages wait to be suburbs;
for factories and terraces to clasp hands.

Bristol swaggers into the eighteenth century, postures
in its expensive suit. It smells
of sugar, cocoa and tobacco. Plantation-picked, ocean fresh.
This Bristol leans from elegant Georgian windows,

dispenses charity with a winning smile.
It hasn't yet learned to dance without crushing others' feet.
It ignores you when you point out the sweat-stains, whistles hymns,
jingles coins in its pockets to drown out the rattle of bones.

Stumble into the nineteenth-century night, follow
the stuttering flames of the linkboy's torch. Arrive in 1817. Gaze up
at the first streetlamp. Bristol shades its eyes,
and squints into an incandescent future.

Bristol marks its place, curates the world, displays it
neatly labelled under glass. The city is a museum,
the museum is a pantry. 200 years of learning
preserved like jam. Unscrew a jar. It still tastes fresh.

Watch – incendiary bombs flicker through the trees,
ghost buildings gather at dusk.
The Blitz gives Bristol the face of an unlucky boxer. In Castle Park
you stumble over rubble until the moment passes. Sirens

soften into laughter, smoke drifts from barbecues and 75 years ago
a fresh wind rushes in. Turn to greet it.
Eyes still bright from Caribbean sun
see Bristol for the first time. The city inhales

their labour, refuses their handshake.
Families hunch their shoulders. Hunker down. Unfurl
new shoots, find hairline cracks in concrete faces,
spread community, grow roots.

At a bus stop in the rain the record skips
back 60 years. Let the buses pass you by. Stand
with your West Indian neighbours as they walk
through spring rains, summer heat

with heads up, with aching feet from double shifts,
with small hands tugging at skirt hems, friends in step, eyes raised until
they walk right through the colour bar
and onto the bus in their new conductors' uniforms.

Bristol buys a ticket, takes a seat, learns to listen and retunes its ears
to 98fm. Light 15 candles for Ujima, for 15 years
sailing the city's airwaves. A lifeboat of Black culture
breaking through storms of white noise.

Bristol coughs and clears its lungs. It's older now, it watches
where it's going, steps a little lighter.
It turns to next century's calendar,
points to the flick-book of blank pages. It tells you –

Close your eyes.
Dream a bridge.
Now

step out.

Introduction

2023 marks the 650th anniversary of Bristol becoming an independent county. This year gives us the opportunity not only to look back at more than six centuries of the city, but also to think about how we might build a better Bristol for the future. This book brings together essays from over 30 contributors, addressing some of the challenges the city faces and sharing ideas about how we might meet them.

There is never just one story of a place. Bristol is a city that holds many contested and contradictory narratives that it tells, or doesn't tell, about itself. Essays by journalist and writer Eugene Byrne and Andrew Kelly, from Bristol Ideas, look at Bristol from its beginnings to 2023. Michael Manson, author of two volumes of *Manson's Bristol Miscellany*, shares his views on the soul of Bristol.

The toppling of the Colston statue is a key part of recent progress, but much more needs to be done in tackling racism and inequality in the city. Using his experience of living in Bath and Bristol, academic Shawn Sobers joins Cleo Lake, former Lord Mayor, to interrogate how much has changed in the past 25 years, the importance of listening and learning, and the potential new step forward with Abolition Shed, a museum that could finally tell the story of the city's history of involvement in the trade in enslaved Africans.

New visions for the city are essential, and sometimes require creative leaps. Former city mayor George Ferguson and business leader Jaya Chakrabarti imagine what Bristol could be like in the 2030s and 2040s. Philosopher Julian Baggini discusses how Bristol can avoid an autonomous future that is unsustainable and unjust.

Other essays in the book highlight Bristol's opportunity to become an exemplary green city. Savita Wilmott, from The Natural History Consortium, explores the city's response to the ecological emergency, writer Pam Beddard shares ideas on what can be done to help nature recover and prosper, and activist Emma Geen writes about the importance of putting justice at the core of environmental work.

Fairness and equality are key themes throughout the book. Dominic Ellison, from WECIL (West of England Centre for Inclusive Living), proposes a future where Bristol is the world's most inclusive city, while Sian Norris interviews a care home owner and a local councillor for their insights into supporting the rising number of adults and children in care. She later lays out why cities need feminism and how we can make Bristol better for women. Geoff Crocker looks at what universal basic income might deliver to people in the city. Alex Raikes and Anna Wardell, from Stand Against Racism and Inequality (SARI), write about building a city with justice at its heart. Annabel Smith, from the Centre for Progressive Policy, draws on her own experience and the wider evidence to show how social mobility has stalled and what can be done to change this. M Winter and Frederick Harry Pitts look at future work through the changes to working patterns on St Philip's Marsh Industrial Estate. Using research gathered from her work, academic Helen Manchester examines how fair and sustainable intergenerational cities are built.

All cities need to invest in new infrastructure. Housing specialist Paul Smith suggests possible answers to the housing crisis. Essays by Louise Delmege, Matty Edwards and Sean Morrison build on *The Bristol Cable*'s City Solutions series to look at how food, transport and energy systems can be transformed. The Covid-19 pandemic and decades of long-term decline and changes in shopping habits have caused a need for renewal of the high street, an issue examined here by writer Jane Duffus.

The city needs new and wider investment, too. Suzanne Rolt, from Quartet Community Foundation, discusses the history of philanthropy in Bristol and the role it might play in the future city. Academic Martin Boddy and Poku Osei, from Babbasa, look at how we can ensure Bristol remains a business centre of excellence, but also becomes a city in which the prosperity created is shared more widely, building a city of aspiration.

The arts and creative industries are critical to making Bristol a good place, and are also important economically. Emma Harvey, from Trinity Centre, writes about beacons of creativity across the city. Journalist Melissa Chemam explores how Bristol's underground and DIY culture prospered in the past and the differences now. Film critic and writer Robin Askew examines the future of filmmaking and exhibition, highlighting the skills shortage currently facing the industry.

In the final section of the book, Evelyn Welch and Steve West – Vice Chancellors at University of Bristol and University of the West of England respectively – discuss the importance of universities to the city and to the economy of the future.

The work of our four City Poets – Miles Chambers, Vanessa Kisuule, Caleb Parkin and Kat Lyons – is featured throughout the book. The role of the City Poets is to reflect on the city and stimulate ideas, as we hope these essays will do.

Bristol is already a city of solutions, and many of the essays highlight good work already underway in the city. We offer these essays in the hope that they will encourage us all to learn more about the city, past and present, provide a guide for thinking about the future, and inspire us all to produce new ideas. We can all help to build a better Bristol. ■

1

BRISTOL TO 2023

1.1

How Bristol Got Here and Some (Possible) Lessons from History

Eugene Byrne

A river, a bridge and a port

'Bristol is well-nigh the most opulent city in the country; admitting merchandise by shipping both from the neighbouring and foreign parts; seated in a very fertile part of England, and, in point of situation, the most impregnable of all the English cities.'
– Gesta Stephani, Anon., twelfth century

Stating the obvious here, but … the port is the key to Bristol's history. That's how Bristol got here, and how it grew. It was a place of trade with the wider world and, equally important (but usually ignored), it was also a place of trade with the rest of the British Isles.

No port, no Bristol. That's it.

Until proper roads came along (Scots engineer John Loudon McAdam pioneered the best ones since Roman times around Bristol in the early 1800s), travel on land was difficult, time-consuming and often dangerous. Ships and boats could move people and things around faster than land travel. Piracy and bad weather notwithstanding, ships, boats and barges were a safer mode of travel than muddy/dusty tracks through bandit-infested Badlands. The sea is not a moat keeping people out. The sea is a highway. Rivers are highways, too.

Bristol started around 1,000 years ago as a bridge over the Avon, deriving its name from the Old English for 'Bridge Place'. The harbour that grew up around this settlement started out trading with neighbouring areas and with Ireland.

By 1400 it was the second (or third) biggest and most important town in England after London and maybe Norwich. Its population was less than 15,000 and its business can be summarised as 'cloth for wine' – woollen cloth was manufactured here and exported in return for wine from France, Spain and Portugal.

Bristol was run by a merchant class which guarded its privileges jealously and which, in 1373, got a charter from the king granting it county status. For the greater part of its history, Bristol was run not by the church or aristocracy, but by an oligarchy of businessmen, which significantly shaped its character.

In the 1490s, geographer Giovanni Caboto (John Cabot) set out from Bristol to cross the 'Ocean Sea' and made landfall in a new-found-land which got called Newfoundland. In the coming centuries, trade would develop between Bristol and North America and the Caribbean. This would, by the later 1600s and well into the 1700s, include dealing in human beings, bought from Africa with Bristol-made trade goods and shipped across the Atlantic to be forced to work, particularly on sugar plantations in the Caribbean, often also owned by Bristol merchant families.

The tidal harbour was converted, at great expense and after a great deal of civic indecision, into a 'floating' one in 1809 – in which there was water all the time – and overseas trade continued expanding into the nineteenth century.

Until Victorian times, ships coming into Bristol were no bigger than many of the white plastic gin palaces moored in the harbour today. As they grew larger, though, the long and winding river approach to the docks became a problem. Vessels frequently grounded on the banks of the Avon, constipating the city's commerce.

Once more, crimson-robed oligarchs debated at great length, looking at the possibility of 'dockising' the river – putting a barrier at or near the Bristol Channel coast to turn the Avon from the city centre to its mouth into an enormous floating harbour. In the end, though, it was judged better to build new docks at the Channel coast, hence Avonmouth and the later additions to the docks complex there.

The city docks in the middle of town were closed to commercial traffic in the later twentieth century and now form the backdrop to housing, pubs, bars, cafés, restaurants, museums and leisure attractions.

Bristol is still a major port; it's just less obvious to most unless you drive over the M5 bridge at Avonmouth and see the acres and acres of imported vehicles waiting there to be sold.

Even in medieval times, Bristol was a cosmopolitan, outward-looking place, a melting pot of cultures and ideas. Also a melting pot of disease and crime, but so it goes...

Immigration

For most of its history, Bristol was bad for your health. Never mind accidents, murders and wars; sickness was always the biggest killer. Disease killed many annually, and tore great lumps out of the population during major epidemics. The Black Death of 1348-50 probably wiped out well over half the inhabitants. Other visitations of plague between then and the later 1600s occasionally carried off a quarter or more of Bristol's people.

By the early 1800s, Bristol numbered around 60,000 souls, and the medieval infrastructure in everything from water supply to housing and even parish graveyards could not cope. This was probably when it was its least healthy; clean water supplies, new sewers and public health measures did much to solve the problem by the 1870s.

Bristol's population and prosperity could only be sustained through immigration to replace the dead and to enable economic expansion. A steady flow of people arriving in search of work is a constant in Bristol's history. Not all newcomers wanted to be there; it seems that there were even enslaved children from Iceland in the Middle Ages.

Most newcomers were from neighbouring counties, or from Ireland or South Wales. There were major waves of immigration from Ireland, Europe and from the former empire and Commonwealth countries after the Second World War and, more recently, from EU countries, especially Eastern Europe.

Bristol has also welcomed asylum seekers, from French Huguenots (Protestants fleeing religious persecution) in the seventeenth century to Belgian refugees in the First World War, and, in the later twentieth and early twenty-first centuries, from many other places, from Vietnam to Iran and Iraq and the Horn of Africa. In the last few years, the largest numbers arriving in Bristol and elsewhere in the UK have come from Hong Kong and Ukraine.

Immigrants and refugees bring new ideas and enterprise. The medieval cloth industry was at least in some degree thanks to Flemish immigrants, while Bristol's glass industry may have been started by Jews, and the cultural and artistic complexion of modern Bristol would have been unthinkable without immigration.

But it was never just about people from overseas. Just as most 'new' Bristolians came from neighbouring counties in previous centuries, most new arrivals now are from elsewhere in the UK, often students who decide to stay after graduating, or because they think Bristol's a cool place to live. It is unusual to hear a Bristol accent among the city's managerial classes; you barely hear it in the council chamber anymore.

Make a list of 50 or 100 'famous Bristolians' in whatever fields you like – business, engineering, academia, the arts, showbiz, sport, politics, whatever – and then dig into their backgrounds. You'll find that over half were either born elsewhere, or that their parents were.

The two truly global 'Bristol' historical celebrities are probably John Cabot (Italian) and Isambard Kingdom Brunel. Brunel's father had fled revolutionary France for his own safety. Brunel, who designed the city's Suspension Bridge, made the railway line to London and built the ss *Great Britain*, was the son of an asylum seeker.

Faith, radicalism and culture wars

One of the hardest things to grasp in our secular age is how utterly all-encompassing the Christian religion was to our forebears. Even as recently as 100 years ago, it was a brave man or woman who stood up to declare themselves an atheist.

In the Middle Ages, the church, headed by the Pope in Rome, was all-powerful and very wealthy. Henry VIII's split with Rome in the 1530s – the English Reformation – had profound consequences in economics and politics as well as religion. Meanwhile, Henry closed down the religious houses and the abbey church of St Augustine became Bristol Cathedral, and so Bristol became a proper city.

Henry and his successors all the way to Charles III were heads of the Church of England. But increasingly, there were other Protestant sects as well. Religion was a key element in the civil wars, the ousting of the Catholic King James II and the arrival of William and Mary in 1688 and, later, the Hanoverian dynasty. Political differences underpinned by religion threatened to spill the country into civil war once more on several occasions in the later 1600s and well into the following century. In Bristol, this factionalism was passionate and often violent.

Bristol became home to a number of 'nonconformist' (because they didn't conform to the Church of England) churches – Quakers, Baptists, Unitarians and others, including the Methodist church founded by the Wesley brothers in the 1700s. Bristol was basically where Methodism began.

Nonconformist churches usually started out with working-class or lower middle-class followers and so, almost by definition, were political dissidents. They all squabbled with one another and often split into sub-groups because of doctrinal differences, but most were united in their dislike and distrust of the Church of England. You can draw a theoretical line connecting, say, the local seventeenth-century puritan troublemaker Dorothy Hazzard (a Baptist) through Quaker campaigners against slavery through First World War conscientious objectors (almost all of whom refused to fight on religious grounds) to today's Bristolian radicals.

Dissenters from any time in the city's past would easily understand what we mean nowadays by 'culture wars', except that their activism was all rooted in their interpretation of the Bible.

Religious nonconformists also founded many of Bristol's biggest business dynasties. Because they were excluded from many conventional professions, some would go on to start successful companies, or become leading innovators, often (in Bristol's case) in medicine and healthcare.

Furthermore, nonconformists were almost all political and/or social activists in their various ways, from abolitionism to the early trade union and labour movements. There also grew a strong tradition of middle-class social activism among many wealthier nonconformist families and churches. Much of this had a strongly religious flavour.

You could also argue that Bristol's former reputation as a rather philistine place which was uninterested in the arts also stemmed from nonconformism's mistrust of pleasure. Because then, as now, radicalism in whatever form can give way to dogma and intolerance.

To understand the differences between the Anglicans and dissenters, visit the Methodist New Room in Broadmead and see how stark and plain it is. Then look at, say, the Anglican Christ Church with St Ewen nearby and see how fabulously ornate and rich it is. Yes, it was about religious belief, but money and politics came into it as well, and some Anglican places of worship were never for the poor.

If you believe that Bristol has a uniquely radical tradition, religious nonconformism is at the root of it.

If you believe that Bristol has an equal and corresponding tradition of conservatism, and complacency, the Church of England is at the root of it. (Not any more; the Church of England nowadays is positively woke by comparison with former times.)

The Victorian explosion

By the time Brunel arrived and work started on his Suspension Bridge in 1831 (the bridge wouldn't be completed until after his death), Bristol was being overtaken in size and economic importance by the great industrial cities of the Midlands and North.

Nonetheless, the city changed beyond all recognition between then and the First World War. Railways and steamships meant commerce grew hugely in scale. Industry expanded, everything from coal mining to engineering, chocolate, tobacco and many other things. Neighbouring Kingswood boasted a huge boot- and shoe-making industry.

By 1901 the population had more than quadrupled to over 320,000. Aside from improved drinking water and sewers, much of this was due to reliable supplies of affordable food, much of it imported.

Whole new suburbs were built. People could live miles from their workplaces and travel to them on trains, or horse-drawn omnibuses and, more usually, trams. The trams were electrified in the 1890s, and on the eve of the First World War, Bristol was building aircraft, and had a fully-fledged university.

We are living through a time of immense change now, but so far it's nothing like the dizzying progress in Bristol in the 50 years before the First World War, which turned the place from a medieval town of wood and stone to a sprawling city of brick and glass.

Technical, social and economic developments created a city we would recognise today, and with all the essential facets of everyday life in place, from commuting to mass-communications. The creation of the modern city, in everything from water and sewers to housing, rail and tram lines, gas and electricity supplies and a sophisticated local government infrastructure, had been a massive challenge, successfully met, though it came at a heavy price in poverty and social dislocation.

Charity

If you were going to be poor in any city in England before the welfare state, Bristol was a pretty good place to be. In the Middle Ages, generations of affluent Bristolians took it as given that they had a religious obligation to help others and gave vast amounts of money to the church and to the poor. Merchant William Canynges (c.1399-1474), one of the richest men in the country, gave up all his wealth to end his days as a priest.

After the Reformation, the rich still gave to charities, much of which benefited the poor, or spent it on philanthropic causes. This compelling sense of obligation continued well into the twentieth century with locally owned companies as well as rich individuals giving back to the community.

While some in recent decades have defended the reputation of slave trader Edward Colston by saying 'how much he did for Bristol', he doesn't stand up to comparison with a lot of others. Aside from his atrocious business dealings, he was a religious bigot who was keen to ensure his bequests only benefited Anglicans.

There are less egregious examples – the Frys, who made their money in chocolate and cocoa, and who were Quakers, gave a great deal. Various members of the Wills dynasty, who got fabulously rich from tobacco, gave away millions to everything from old people's homes to the University of Bristol. Victorian mining magnate Handel Cossham (1824-1890) built an entire hospital.

(All of which assumes you can square away the fact that many businesses benefited directly or indirectly from enslaved labour or exploited their workforces or, as in the Wills case, got millions addicted to a killer drug. Behind every great fortune is a great crime, and all that.)

Globalism has severed ties between commerce and community, though the Society of Merchant Venturers, a commercial lobby group founded in Tudor times which now claims to be purely philanthropic, might argue that it leads the way locally in charity – running schools in deprived areas, for example.

Part of the reason behind the bizarre 'cult of Colston' espoused both by Liberals (whom he would have despised) and by Tories in the nineteenth century was that he was supposed to show how the kindness of rich men was better than socialism.

While increasing prosperity and a growing diversity of industries created a large middle class, it created an even bigger working class whose lives were often precarious, and who sought to improve pay and working conditions by forming or joining trade unions. Towards the late 1800s and early 1900s there were a number of increasingly bitter and sometimes violent industrial disputes. Bristol spawned two of the giants of the early Labour movement, Ben Tillett (1860-1943) and Ernest Bevin (1881-1951).

"We are living through a time of immense change now, but so far it's nothing like the dizzying progress in Bristol in the 50 years before the First World War..."

There was also a large underclass living in appalling slum conditions, most of them in central areas of the city, and whose lives were often blighted by alcoholism. Bristol was a bastion of the temperance movement, which tried to get people to swear off drink.

While Bristol was a regional stronghold of the political left, it was also a significant centre of middle-class social activism, of people going into deprived communities and slums to try and improve people's lives, whether through education or religion. Women were at the forefront of this movement. Some were preachy and evangelical, but others, such as Mabel Tothill (1869-1964), Hilda Cashmore (1876-1943) or Marian Pease (1859-1954) – founders of the University Settlement at Barton Hill – made a real difference to people's lives. Some, you might argue, such as Hannah More (1745-1833) or Mary Carpenter (1807-1877), fell somewhere in between ....

Decades of social activism by well-connected women led to growing demands for women's education and women's right to vote. Bristol was one of the UK's leading centres of agitation for women's suffrage. With a few exceptions, the leadership locally of this movement was overwhelmingly middle class.

Much attention is paid in present-day Bristol to the suffrage campaigners, but in 1918 the less affluent third or so of the *male* population finally got the vote (along with women over 30 subject to various conditions). This had significant consequences.

In the febrile political atmosphere between the wars, when socialist revolution seemed a real possibility, Bristol's Tory and Liberal councillors dissolved centuries of mutual loathing overnight, combining as the 'Citizen Party'. By gaming the system, they kept Labour out of power in the Council House until 1938. Since then, Labour has controlled the council more often than not.

Engineering and innovation

Nineteenth- and twentieth-century industries were made possible by new technologies adapted by Bristol. The most successful entrepreneurs tended not to invent much.

You can see this in the career of Sir George White (1854-1916), who took an American invention to revolutionise his Bristol trams by electrifying them, and who then set out to build an aviation industry, rejecting experiment in favour of using proven ideas from elsewhere. The hugely successful Wills cigarette industry was based on the licensing of American manufacturing technology. The small but prestigious Bristol car company started out with designs 'liberated' from Germany at the end of the Second World War.

Brunel never invented much himself but adapted new ideas, though his perfectionism ended up driving almost every project over budget.

Few significant inventions came out of Victorian Bristol; there was the mass-produced hollow chocolate Easter Egg (Frys, 1873, or so it's claimed) and self-raising flour (Welsh-born Broadmead baker Henry Jones, 1845), but in later times the city has been a home of considerable innovation, particularly in aviation and aerospace.

Bristol can also make many claims to innovation in a field that's generally overlooked – medicine, from pioneering treatments of mental illness to more recent work on paramedics thanks in large part to Frenchay Hospital anaesthetist Peter Baskett (1934-2008). American-born neuroscientist William Grey Walter (1910-1977) built some of the world's first robots in the 1940s, while Inmos at Aztec West developed some of the earliest semiconductors in the 1970s.

The decline of the manufacturing industry has been accompanied by the rise in Bristol's 'knowledge economy' in recent decades, often linked to the universities, with developments in IT, medicine, materials technology, communications and media.

The modern Bristol brand

The First World War accounted for 7,000-8,000 Bristolian dead in the fighting services and merchant marine and in the influenza pandemic of 1918-1919, which was a direct result of the war. In itself, however, the war did not dramatically change the cityscape or the economy.

The Second World War saw large areas laid waste as a result of enemy bombing. After the war, city planners wrought an immense amount of change. Castle Park was created from what had been a dense retail and residential area; the Broadmead shopping centre was built in the 1950s and numerous road schemes followed. There was also a massive council house-building programme which took thousands of families from cramped and insanitary housing out to new estates, mostly on the city's fringes.

Most of Bristol's trademark manufacturing industries were closing by the 1980s. Sometime around this period Bristol started to change character, going from a sober, hard-working place to a new identity as a creative, 'alternative', hedonistic and frequently riotous place.

All UK cities reinvented themselves in the post-industrial age, turning former docks into destinations (Manchester, Liverpool, Portsmouth, Cardiff etc.) and former industrial buildings into apartments. What is arguably different about Bristol is the growth of the importance of arts, entertainment and media – from Aardman Animations to Banksy and the 'Bristol Sound' – in a place which, despite a few outliers (e.g. the early nineteenth-century 'Bristol School' of artists) was never seen as particularly cultured.

By the 1990s the city was gaining a worldwide reputation, especially in music, clubs and free parties and street art. In more recent times, it's possible that the hedonism has been sidelined by a more sober political/social activism.

The demographics have changed, too. Bristol is undoubtedly more diverse ethnically, but also often segregated into different neighbourhoods. There are also 40,000-plus students in Bristol in term-time, threatening to turn other areas into monocultures.

The public image, the brand peddled even by the city council, is in any event at odds with reality. For all the computer games designers, pop-up shops, the protests and the historic toppling of Colston, most of the population go about their business, many struggling to make ends meet.

Are we really that different from Victorian Bristol – a small upper crust, a large middle class, a precarious blue-collar class, and a large and hidden underclass?

So ... some themes to argue about

'History never repeats itself, but it does often rhyme.'
– Mark Twain

'Thee's got'n whur thee casn't back'n, assn't?'
– Adge Cutler

What do we have in common with Bristolians from 200 years ago, 500 years ago or more? People who lived in a place mostly built of wood and stone, travelled on horses or wooden sailing ships (but mostly on foot), who all believed in the Christian God?

Or even just the Bristolians of 100 years ago; folk who mostly worked in manufacturing and paid lip-service, at least, to the Christian God? A city where almost everyone considered meat essential to their diet, where Black people were so unusual that if mothers saw one they'd tell their children to touch them for luck? A place where the working classes spoke not just in a local accent, but a now almost-forgotten dialect?

Most of our grandparents were born somewhere else. All we have in common with previous inhabitants is that we simply occupy the same patch of Planet Earth, right?

And yet there are ghosts and resonances lurking in those old stones, bricks and timbers; themes and constants which maybe continue to shape the city today. For instance:

- **Immigration is key,** whether it's from Wales, the Home Counties or the far side of the world. Bristol has always needed to bring people in.

- **Bristolian exceptionalism.** There was always a strong sense of local autonomy even in the Middle Ages, and many still feel the place is different today.

- **Rule by oligarchy.** For much of its history Bristol, reasonably distant from royal control, was run by businessmen. Even twentieth-century Labour party councillors and Lord Mayors often also held office in trade unions and/or public service bodies. In the 1700s only a minority of the population were allowed to vote; in local elections in recent decades only a minority bothered to vote. This is no different from most other cities, but it suggests that the present-day radical brand is perhaps exaggerated. Bristol's first Green Party councillor wasn't elected until 2006.

- **Middle-class activism.** Bristol produced many working-class labour leaders and giants of the labour movement but they were focussed on the immediate needs of those they represented, usually simply pay and conditions. It has also been represented in Parliament by two megastars of Labour's left, Stafford Cripps (1889-1952) and Tony Benn (1925-2014). New immigrant communities also concentrated on immediate needs, such as the 1963 bus boycott over employment rights. But an unusually large bourgeois minority spearheaded many campaigns, from the anti-slavery movement in the 1700s/1800s to suffragism in the 1800s/1900s. How much present-day activism is predominantly middle-class in character?

- **Endless culture wars.** Left and right, Anglican and nonconformist, Roundhead and Cavalier, Whig and Tory ... to modern day cyclists vs motorists or Colston apologists vs statue-drowners. When the Royalists captured Bristol in 1643, they taunted the defeated Roundheads, we're told, mimicking them by speaking in the same, sneering, high-pitched, nasal tones that we use to mock killjoys almost 400 years later.

  While many like to claim Bristol has usually/always been on the progressive side of history, the city has – or used to have – a corresponding tradition of conservatism. The Tories ran the council for the entire nineteenth century, and those who campaigned to keep slavery or deny women the vote only got written out of history because they lost – but there were plenty of them.

- **Dithering.** Indecision and delay over major infrastructure projects is a fine old Bristolian tradition, from the floating harbour in the eighteenth century to dockisation in the nineteenth. Fast-forward to the present, and the Arena has been on the drawing board since 2003, while studying public transport plans since the 1980s is strictly for masochists, or fans of job-creation schemes for consultants. In 2023, with plans for the 'Bristol Underground' hitting the buffers, Mayor Rees slammed the city and wider region for 'lack of ambition'.

  And yet when Bristol has been ambitious, the results have been spectacular. The post-Second World War plans were on a vast scale and though they gave us some hideous concrete office blocks, the plan overall, implemented more slowly than the planners would have liked, gave tens of thousands decent housing and was the backdrop to major advances in living standards. The tram system in the nineteenth century smoothed the way for immense growth, and by 1900 was one of the most modern, and envied, in the world.

  Some more of that would be nice. ∎

Eugene Byrne is a Bristol-based author, historian and journalist. He has written several books on Bristol's history, including *The Bristol Story* (with artist Simon Gurr) and a brief history of council housing in Bristol (with artist Anthony Forbes). He edits the *Bristol Post*'s 'Bristol Times' local history pull-out.

Q Explore the history of Bristol with a visit to M Shed
www.bristolmuseums.org.uk/m-shed/

1.2

What Will Be the Long-Term Impact of the Years 2020-2023 in Bristol?

Andrew Kelly

How will future generations look back on the years 2020-2023 in Bristol? What long-term impact did the Covid-19 pandemic have? Did the defeat of the mayoral system usher in new forms of democracy, greater levels of trust in politics and politicians and wider civic engagement? Did pulling down the Colston statue lead to less inequality and racism?

Taking a pessimistic view, the potential improvements that the pandemic might have ushered in – or started – did not happen, or at least have not happened yet. The fractures in society that were there before 2020 were made worse. The inability to solve long-running problems continued – in relation to social care, house prices and rents, inequality and social mobility and the future of work, among other areas. Added to these were a cost-of-living crisis, a worsening environmental emergency, where national and international action seemed more limited than ever, and a war in Ukraine which grew more frightening by the month.

Change can be slow and is often the work of decades. At times it needs to be fast, and the pandemic response – for all its faults and with lessons to be learned – showed that swift action could be taken in the face of a crisis. But the will, imagination and investment needed for wider change failed to be adopted. It is no wonder that many felt that everything had broken, and we began to hear the term polycrisis, highlighting the multiple and interconnecting crises we face.

There are lessons to learn from these three years for the Bristol of the future and for cities elsewhere. Essays in this collection address some of the challenges faced by the city and put forward new ideas. Here, I look at the pandemic and the way the city council led the response, the future of democracy and reckoning with the past.

***

The pandemic stay-at-home order meant deserted streets. Getting to work in Bristol, for those allowed to do so, was easy, if unnerving and sometimes frightening. In the council, there were few people in City Hall and much of the ground floor was filled with Personal Protective Equipment and food packages.

According to the UK government dashboard, Covid-19 was referred to on 929 death certificates issued in Bristol between March 2020 and the end of June 2023. How prepared was Bristol and how local was the response? Our over-centralised state meant that much of the action was driven nationally. People leading the response here often heard news at the same time as those listening to the national press conferences. Bristol's public health system, however, was well organised, and through the City Office and the One City Boards, brought together civic, community and faith groups to work collaboratively.

I was one of thousands of people who had a family member die alone when Covid-19 restrictions were in place. It was a bleak time. However, despite all the problems and the horror, there were good things to emerge. Mutual aid was strong in places; communication was clear and geared towards reaching all communities in the city (essential in a place where 91 languages are spoken); and the vaccine team continued to be praised into 2023, especially for work with minority ethnic communities. This was the finest moment for the City Office. If it had not already existed it would have had to have been invented quickly as it was invaluable and a model for others.

Wider changes were also to be welcomed: working from home allowed more time with family and less traffic; the use of pavements and roads for cafés and restaurants, when allowed to open, provided a different feel to city centres; the air felt cleaner and there seemed to be more insects and birdsong; and some free time allowed – during the official exercise period – the chance to explore cities more. Some of these improvements did not last, however.

The pandemic has longer-term implications which may take decades to work through. The impact on the economy has been huge and has put further pressure on government finances. We may not have seen the end of cities – which was one of the fears – but we have damaged cities, with empty office blocks and further declining shopping centres. The impact on culture has continued into 2023, with venues fearing permanently reduced audience attendance. Education for young people and students was interrupted and there are fears nationally that some children have opted out of school altogether. Loneliness – a serious problem before the pandemic – is likely to have worsened. And trust in politicians and national government has declined further, especially after Partygate.

It is doubtful that the national Covid-19 inquiry will address all these issues. My proposal for a local inquiry failed to get any support but it is essential that there is learning and change, not just for the next pandemic but also to prepare cities for the other challenges they face, especially in updated resilience strategies. And national government needs to recognise the greater efficiency and effectiveness of acting locally and extend devolution further permanently, not just during future pandemics.

***

Dealing with the pandemic has been one battle. Bristol was also involved in a fight over its future governance: first in May 2021, with the third mayoral election, and then, a year later, with the referendum on the mayoral system. On a turnout of just over 41 per cent Marvin Rees won his second election with 59,276 votes. Sandy Hore-Ruthven for the Greens ran him close, receiving 45,663 votes, and it went to two rounds. The turnout in 2012, when independent candidate George Ferguson won, was just under 28 per cent, though in 2021 the mayoral election took place alongside other local elections, which might explain the higher percentage. In May 2021, Labour's Dan Norris was elected the West of England Combined Authority mayor on a turnout of 36.6 per cent.

Twelve months on, Bristol voted to return the council to a committee system. A turnout of just under 29 per cent saw 38,439 favour a directly elected mayor with 56,113 preferring a committee system. Turnout was up by around five percentage points in comparison to the first referendum in 2012.

Low turnout – having fewer than a third voting in the referendum – was not good for democracy. It was a poor debate, tending to focus on the incumbent mayor, Marvin Rees. Unlike the referendum a decade earlier, there was no cross-party campaign for the mayoral system. There was little interest nationally: media coverage was limited, and national journalists who should have been better informed did not know it was taking place. Locally there was confusion: no explanatory booklet was sent to households and some people I spoke to thought that their polling cards were for a normal council election. There was only one city-wide debate. A group of academics provided neutral background information but, in the end, did people really have enough information to cast a vote? No wonder turnout was low.

The pro-committee campaign was better organised and targeted voters well, and was helped by George Ferguson, the first elected mayor, coming out in favour of abolishing the post. It did have campaigners from all parties and had momentum from the start, led by a dynamic organiser. The resurgent Green Party helped too, even though its mayoral candidate wanted the post to continue. He may have won if there had been another election. In 2023 the Greens became the largest party on Bristol City Council following a (bad-tempered) by-election for the Hotwells and Harbourside seat. Turnout there was 32.4 per cent.

The mayoral model was flawed from the start. There were no significant extra resources. There was confusion between the roles of the ceremonial mayor and the elected mayor. The introduction of a mayor for the West of England Combined Authority added to the confusion and the relationship between city and combined authority mayor was troubled. Once power was centralised, the role of councillors outside of the cabinet was limited. Being leader of the city and chief advocate meant participation in national conferences and international visits were essential, though these were sometimes criticised as not being necessary.

There were positives. It led, sometimes, to faster decision-making and both of the elected mayors put Bristol on the international map more than ever before. In the future, mayors may be seen to have delivered more than they are given credit for now. But there were many controversial decisions too: moving the proposed arena to the old Brabazon site was seen by some as decisive, by others as a betrayal of the plans for the city centre; growing investment in Bristol Beacon took place at the same time as reductions in general cultural funding; and the Bristol Energy debacle saw the council apologise for the high costs.

Were there other options that might have been explored? Attempts to review the role of the mayor through a Green Party motion went nowhere (as did a proposal from the mayor's office to have a review – Mayor at 10). There were justified calls for a rainbow cabinet – or just red and green – when Labour lost seats on the council. And there seem to have been discussions about a leader and cabinet model, though the referendum was limited to a binary choice so only the committee system was put forward. Bristol should have had a Citizens' Assembly on this to help people decide and promote a sustained debate and better deliberation. The result may not have been different, but the process of decision-making would have been better. Would anyone bet against another referendum in 2032?

I have worked within a committee system, a cabinet and leader and a directly elected mayor. Each has its benefits and challenges. We made progress under a committee system on Harbourside, especially with the development of At-Bristol (now We the Curious). The bid for 2008 Capital of Culture started in the last days of the committee system. Approval to bid was given, but reluctantly. After shortlisting there was better leadership, and the judges were impressed by Diane Bunyan, the council leader at that time. The cabinet and leader model that followed offered support for the bid until the council went hung. The absence of leadership then hampered the last stage with judges questioning whether the council could deliver. A mayor would have been helpful here, though a leader would have worked too.

***

Despite the low turnout and a poor debate in May 2022, democracy did win and plans for the new system are in development. However, although we are not at the level of Hong Kong, Turkey, Russia and many other places where democracy is under serious attack (thinking about these places made me wince over accusations of Bristol being run by a dictatorship), we urgently need democratic renewal in both Bristol and the UK, especially if we are to build a free and fair society and to reverse some of the populist trends we have encountered in recent years. Changes to city governance should just be the start. We have let democracy slip over the decades, and it may take the work of decades more to recover.

There is a long list of things to do – big and small; short-term and well into the future; some needing national change, others where local action is possible. These – taken from interviews for this essay – include:

- Rebuilding trust in institutions (though there is more trust in local than national politicians).
- Abolition of the House of Lords and the creation of an elected second chamber.
- Greater use of Citizens' Assemblies.
- Votes at 16.
- Electoral reform.
- Greater openness and transparency.
- Local bodies that are representative.
- Greater engagement, without putting off those already engaged.
- Devolved funding with the discretion to spend locally, not taking instructions from someone in London who rarely visits.
- Ensuring scrutiny works.
- Building capacity for local decision-making for local services. In the past 15 years Bristol City Council has gone from having a budget of £650 million and 14,000 staff to £380 million and 6,000 staff (this includes teachers who were taken out of the authority, but it still shows a substantial reduction with parks and planning affected especially).
- Making sure that councillors have all the information they need to make decisions, which might mean more political support.
- Ensuring full council meetings are fora for debate and decision-making.
- Building learning about democracy and governance into school education.
- Encouraging wider reporting about civic matters, though the state of local newspapers, the lack of resources for local news sources and the row over local democracy reporters being allowed to attend mayoral press conferences shows how far we have to go.

We need better debate and deliberation, too. The rise of social media and binary referenda questions have seen increased polarisation, the loss of nuance and the loss of the idea that we can still talk to each other even when we disagree.

We will all need to navigate and discuss issues better, whether it is green growth, the car vs public transport, housing in the green belt, low-traffic neighbourhoods, pedestrianisation, tall buildings, airport expansion, the climate crisis and what we will need to do, in addition to the other challenges we face.

Renewing democracy and engaging more people are not easy tasks. For many people, interest in the local council is limited to whether the bins are emptied, and potholes fixed. Recent referenda on Brexit and the Scottish independence vote achieved large turnouts, but most other elections fail to arouse similar interest. We should never be happy with a turnout of less than 30 per cent on a subject as important as the future governance of the city, even if that was a small improvement on the referendum vote a decade before.

Work on further devolution of powers and funding now moves to the West of England Combined Authority. The 2023 trailblazer deals agreed with Greater Manchester and the West Midlands show what is possible, though in these cases are just a start. A West of England deal like the ones achieved by others becomes the next important step forward. Without it, Bristol and the West of England will fail to prosper and will not have the opportunity to become fairer and better places to live, work in and visit. And, like elsewhere, this should be just the start of maximising the potential of devolution.

***

There was progress on Bristol dealing with its past. Sparked by Black Lives Matter protests, the Colston statue was toppled and ended up in the docks in June 2020. The failure to deal with the statue for decades – through inaction and with initiatives often blocked in the city – and recent attempts to produce an alternative plaque to explain more about the man and his work (this should not have been hard, but it was) left a bitterness among many. That it happened how and when it did was surprising to some, and it was also surprising to some that the Colston Four were later acquitted. Though he could not condone law-breaking, the mayor was right to say there was poetic justice in the statue ending in the dock, and though he was criticised – both for failing to defend the statue as well as for taking down the alternatives put up – his response, which can be seen in the 2021 BBC documentary *Statue Wars: One Summer in Bristol*, is likely to be regarded as a high point in his term of office. For a time, the eyes of the world were on Bristol and city leadership delivered.

In the years just before the statue was toppled, more had been done to address the city's past role in the trade in enslaved people and its continuing legacy. However, this did not provoke the reckoning that was needed. The Bristol Bus Boycott leaders began to be recognised more nationally and were celebrated locally with the Seven Saints of St Paul's project, finished in 2019. September 2020 saw the formal announcement of the name change of Colston Hall to Bristol Beacon, though this had been signalled in 2017 when it was announced that its reopening after extensive refurbishment would be accompanied by a new name. There was education work led by CARGO and Project T.R.U.T.H. (Telling, Restoring, Understanding our Tapestry and History) and talk of a Bristol curriculum, among other initiatives. No one could be in any doubt about Colston following the publication (in the same month as the statue came down) of

From Wulfstan to Colston: Severing the Sinews of Slavery in Bristol by Mark Steeds and Roger Ball, though other damning material had been published well before 2020 and more has emerged since.

It is likely that the toppling of Colston will be seen as one of the key moments in Bristol's history in the decades to come. What immediately followed the statue coming down included changes to school names, the replacement of commemorative windows in Bristol Cathedral and St Mary Redcliffe Church and much soul searching. The Society of Merchant Venturers commissioned new research into their links with the trade in enslaved people. What has not yet been solved are long-running problems of racism, inequality and fairness.

In 2023 there were significant signs of progress but also a crashing reality about what still faced the city. The fact that key civic leaders – Bishop of Bristol, High Sheriff, Lord Lieutenant, Vice-Chancellor of the University of Bristol – were women, and two of these women of colour, was positive news. However, in June 2023, and based on the criteria set by Baroness Casey in her report into the Met Police, Chief Constable Sarah Crew said, 'Avon and Somerset Police is institutionally racist.' Creating a city that is fair and more equal will be the true legacy of the Colston statue coming down.

***

Change in Bristol can be disruptive. Often opposition to change is justified given the disastrous plans of the past. We are no different from other places, although we should be demanding more. To meet what is coming, the city will need to continue to change. It will need help – more powers, including greater ability to raise funds locally – but it will also need greater involvement in the city's future from the people of Bristol.

I was born just at the end of the baby boomer period and have had the advantages of that group. I was a beneficiary of the belief – the understanding, even – that my generation would, at least most of us, be better off than our parents and that the generations that followed would continue to prosper. Those 30 glorious years after the Second World War of social mobility, better productivity and growing wages faltered in the 1970s and that generational promise has ended. We need that promise back. We can learn from this past. But it is what comes next that counts. ■

Andrew Kelly is Creative Programmer at Bristol Ideas, having previously been its director. He is a visiting professor at the University of the West of England and has written books on subjects ranging from Hollywood film and cinema to Brunel, aviation and Bristol's rich cultural history.

1.3

The Soul of the City: A Personal View

Michael Manson

I arrived in Bristol the week that Arnolfini moved to its present location on Narrow Quay. It was October 1975 and Bristol was on the cusp of change. Arnolfini stood in an empty harbour landscape. Apart from a sand dredger berthed in Bathurst Basin, the docks were deserted and eerily quiet. As I sipped my lapsang souchong tea – this was in the days before flat whites – Bristol felt different. I liked the West Country feel. The florid faces in cider pubs; the gentle accent; the jazz in King Street. For me, brought up in the Home Counties, the West meant one thing – holidays.

I did what every newcomer to Bristol should do. I climbed the 108 steps to the top of Cabot Tower, which had been erected in 1897 to mark the 400th anniversary of Cabot's pioneering voyage to North America. The rolling topography of Bristol is spread below the tower. To the west, Clifton's Georgian terraces are stacked up the hillside. Then there's a glimpse of Brunel's Suspension Bridge, while the flag-clad masts of the ss *Great Britain* poke up from the docks. There's the cathedral and the elegant spire of St Mary Redcliffe. You can make out the tower blocks of Hartcliffe, huddling below the Dundry slopes and the landmark Dundry church tower. The 1930s estate of Knowle West is tucked over the ridge. The north of the city is largely obscured by the steep drama of St Michael's Hill.

The 1970s was a time of rising unemployment. I wasn't sure what I could do with my sociology degree. There was one place I reckoned I could get a job: the dole office in Nelson Street. It was a sharp introduction to Bristol at its rawest, and was to be the setting for my book *Where's My Money?* (2016). *Where's My Money?* is fiction – I have to say this as I'd signed the Official Secrets Act. Working in the dole office was a good way to discover the less celebrated side of Bristol. I met shifters, grifters and the early morning snifters. But mostly it was hard-working people down on their luck.

Several years later, when I was dating Maggie, my future wife, she was alarmed by how many street drinkers knew me.

I quickly got to discover the city. It wasn't London. It didn't feel like London, it didn't look to London. Bristol has been called the capital of the South West. I'm not so sure about that. I don't think a Cornish person would see it that way. Nevertheless, Bristol has traditionally looked westwards, away from the capital.

Historically, Bristol owes its existence to its harbour. At first sight, the twisting Avon, with its ferocious tidal range, is a strange location for a port. But it was safe. There would never be a surprise attack on Bristol by water.

During medieval times there was significant trade with Ireland and even Iceland. And then came trade with North America. Few were surprised in 1497 when John Cabot came across a supposedly new continent – new to Europeans, at least. Canny Bristolians knew of a faraway land with a cod-rich sea well before Cabot's voyage.

Today the docks are quiet. Commercial shipping has moved to easier moorings at the mouth of the Avon. But Bristol's past links with the sea are still in evidence. Waterside warehouses have been repurposed for arts centres, cafés, nightclubs and museums. The sculptural cranes are heritage pieces. Even the Underfall Yard with its sluices, vital for the regulation of the water level of the harbour, is a working museum. Sadly, it has recently suffered a devastating fire. Rather than taking labourers to work, ferries now scoot tourists across the harbour. The docks may well have closed for commercial trade, but the harbour remains an unmistakable emblem of Bristol. On a warm summer's evening there are few better places to be.

Bristol's motto is *Virtute et Industria* – virtue and industry. *Industria* maybe, but *virtute*, certainly not. If we understand virtue to mean 'high moral standards', over the years Bristol's merchants have fallen tragically short. The transatlantic trade in enslaved people that dominated Bristol's commerce for over 150 years gave the city great wealth. But at what human cost? Between 1698 and 1807 it is estimated that over half a million kidnapped Africans were transported by Bristol's ships. The barbarity of this enterprise is almost too horrendous to countenance. It is history that cannot be ignored and is currently being unearthed and rewritten. Directly or indirectly the effects of slavery are all pervading.

Bristol is said to be a city of protest; Bristolians demand to be listened to. In *The Bristol Guide*, printed and published by Joseph Mathews in the early 1800s, it is written that 'the populace are apt to collect in mobs on the slightest and most frivolous occasions'. But riots aren't the only way of showing discontent. In the 1960s, Bristol Omnibus Company, jointly administered by Bristol City Council, operated a blatant colour bar. The Bristol Bus Boycott in 1963 influenced the passing of Britain's first Race Relations Act two years later.

It was a proud moment when Bristol hit the world news in June 2020. A statue of Edward Colston, a Bristol-born slave trader, was pulled down, rolled along the waterfront and dumped into the docks. For several years there had been discussions regarding the text of a plaque to explain the origins of Colston's wealth. But little had happened. Wording was agreed and rejected. Eventually, during a Black Lives Matter protest, the demonstrators took things into their own hands.

Rescued from its watery grave, for a while the Colston statue, splattered with red paint, lay recumbent on display in M Shed museum. While it is no longer on show, the statue can be viewed on M Shed behind-the-scenes tours.

You can't help but notice that Bristol is a youthful city. With two universities and a student population of over 40,000 there's a constant flow of new talent to support Bristol's world-class creative industries. There's a myth that Bristol is laid back. Don't be fooled. Bristol may not be a city of sharp suits and overly aggressive businesspeople but there's a heroic energy to the place.

Concorde, the BBC Studios Natural History Unit and bad-boy-turned-saviour Banksy are internationally known. We have Paul Dirac to thank for Quantum Physics and, at the other end of the spectrum, who doesn't love Wallace and Gromit? I could go on. For a city of just under half a million people Bristol punches well above its weight.

However, as I saw when I worked in the dole office, there is darker side to the city. In 2017, drawing on data from the 2001 and 2011 censuses, the Runnymede Trust produced a report that revealed Bristol to be more unequal than most other UK cities. Far from being a melting pot of diversity and multiculturalism the report (*Bristol: A City Divided?*) found that Bristol's Black and Minority Ethnic communities had poorer job prospects, worse health and fewer academic qualifications than those in the white communities. What the report didn't mention is that there are white communities in Bristol that are also living in areas of deprivation. Bristol has a problem. Positive action is required.

One last thing. Here's a question you should never ask in Bristol. 'How do I get to...?' Even before the current Clean Air Zone restrictions, this is a query that strikes dread in the hearts of Bristolians. Bristol has grown organically, there's no grand planning, no grids of streets. The city is sliced not only by the Avon but also The Cut. Then there are the vertiginous hills. Bristol has some of the steepest residential streets in the UK. There is no direct route anywhere. The quickest way to get from A to B is open to constant debate. Don't bother with sat nav – it has no idea, either.

I've lived in Bristol for nearly 50 years and I still feel I'm on holiday. I continue to explore the city, finding new corners, new streets, new communities, even. There's a vitality to the city and always something new to try. Want late night music? Try the grimy buzz of Stokes Croft. Looking for off-the-wall art? Go to the fabulously bohemian annual Totterdown Arts Trail (other arts trails are available). Searching for exotic food? Visit the multicultural St Mark's Road, Easton. Keen to see epic street art? Make your way to North Street, Bedminster. And when you're tired of all that you can take an energising stroll in one of Bristol's many attractive parks and marvel (sometimes) at the hot air balloons floating overhead.

My career has been Bristol-based and, with my wife, I've brought up two children in the city. With its enterprising, creative and free-thinking people and its unique geography, I can't think of a better place to have done this. ∎

Michael Manson was a co-editor of the *Bristol Review of Books* (2006-13), a co-founder of the Bristol Short Story Prize (2008) and an organiser of the Bristol Festival of Literature (2010-2020). He currently edits Bristol Civic Society's *Better Bristol* magazine. He is the author of six history books and three published novels, including *Manson's Bristol Miscellany* Volumes One and Two.

> 🔍 Climb the 108 steps of the Cabot Tower to experience the view of Bristol described here. https://visitbristol.co.uk/things-to-do/cabot-tower-and-brandon-hill-p24401

"I continue to explore the city, finding new corners, new streets, new communities, even. There's a vitality to the city and always something new to try."

1.4

Why Bristol Needs to Face Its History to Move Forward

Shawn-Naphtali Sobers

I grew up in Bath in the 1970s and 1980s. After studying in Newport, I moved to Bristol in 1996. I was drawn to Bristol because of the creative community I found there, especially at Kuumba Centre, the African Caribbean cultural arts space in St Pauls. While on work experience at Black Pyramid Films, I got involved with other projects, including the Bristol Black Writers group. It felt like home and, after graduating, I returned to Bristol and made it so.

As a child, I often came to Bristol with my family, mainly for shopping. It was more affordable than Bath. Later, I'd regularly travel up the A4 with friends for the nightclubs, St Pauls Carnival, and other entertainment, and be back in Bath for daily life. I often observed how, like us Bathonians, tourists would usually stay in Bath, travel to Bristol for the day or night, then retreat back to the Roman city for the remainder of their stay. It was around 2000, when I was working for At-Bristol (now We The Curious), that I saw this begin to reverse, and Bristol started to attract more of its own tourists. They'd visit Bath for the day for sightseeing and then return to the bigger city for more variety.

Bath is proud of its Roman and Georgian history and architecture, and it can take a generation for any innovative planning decisions to be made, as the council's mind is primarily on the city's UNESCO status and wants to avoid disruption to the world-renowned landscape. In contrast, when I came to Bristol, so much development was happening. It felt like buildings were being knocked down and modern replacements were rising from the dust before we even realised a planning application had been submitted.

Bath has built its reputation on a confident historical narrative of Romans and Georgians, and this can sometimes feel stifling to residents. Bristol's lack of a dominant historical narrative makes for more of a patchwork cultural landscape (Brunel, Concorde, music, rebellion, slavery), and its approach to telling its history is often one made up of temporary initiatives, rather than permanent markers, with some notable exceptions. You have two cities – one wedded to the past, and the other seemingly marching into the future.

The use of temporary initiatives is nowhere truer than in how Bristol's involvement in transatlantic slavery has been dealt with. As the city moved forward, there was tension with those who were demanding the slavery story was told in full. This tension and growing energy convinced the Bristol City Museum to host the 'A Respectable Trade' exhibition in 1999, which, for the first time, saw the city get behind telling the story of its slave-trading history. Rob Mitchell and I produced the HTV documentary *Under the Bridge* about the feelings in the city during that time, and interviewed artist Tony Forbes about his self-portrait, 'Sold Down the River', which was commissioned for the exhibition.

Tony told us: 'I wanted to truthfully address the problems what I went through in Bristol, and I looked at a time when I felt really angry and ashamed with the city on the issue of race ... In the painting you see me on a raft floating down a river, with the Colston statue behind me holding me with chains ... I'm being dragged under the Suspension Bridge, and you see the silhouette of people dancing on the bridge, councillors, people in the media organisations, whose logos are represented on the sails of the boat, having a party while I'm being dragged into an oblivion.'

Tony's painting and words managed to articulate what many of the city's African heritage citizens were feeling – that there had been a wilful neglect from the city leaders to formally acknowledge this history, or to accept the connection with present-day inequalities in society. Visitor numbers exceeded any the museum had experienced before and the exhibition was hailed as a success. A small number of the exhibits, including Tony's painting, were displayed in the M Shed museum when it opened 12 years later.

Some say the city has never dealt with its slave-trading history, but (even though I'm fearful of being misquoted) I would argue that is not true. In the 24 years since 'A Respectable Trade', there have been plenty of funded projects relating to the city's connection with transatlantic slavery, including exhibitions, films, theatre performances, poetry, talks and panel discussions. However, they have all been temporary initiatives, not permanent, which gives rise to the accusation that the city continually sweeps the topic under the carpet. It's a fair criticism, and it is this tension of temporary versus permanence, and the frustration of a lack of long-term visibility in acknowledging its slaving past, that in part fuelled the toppling of the Colston statue in 2020. Tony Forbes' painting unsurprisingly took on extra resonance at that time. We pointed to it, saying, 'See, this hasn't come from nowhere, we've been trying to say this for at least the past 21 years.'

What will the conversation be in 24 years' time? 2047 might seem difficult to comprehend, but it feels like just yesterday that Rob and I were interviewing Tony for our film, and in those interim years the conversation feels largely the same: 'How is the city dealing meaningfully with its slavery history and present-day inequality?'. It is now time to take meaningful action. There are renewed calls for a permanent site in the city where this history can be explored and for enslaved Africans to be commemorated. There are strong signs that the mayoral leadership agrees with the plans, and I will do all I can to support the work. I am reminded of Rob's provocative words at the end of our documentary, his words still relevant today:

'So there's now an exhibition in the city about Bristol and the transatlantic slave trade. It feels like there should be some sort of conclusion at this point, but there's still too many questions to be asked. So what next? Because this is not the end, but the start of a healing process. But is there such a thing as too much healing? Can the situation ever be cured? Are we just picking a wound and making it worse? Will there ever be a time that we can close this chapter? What more can we do with this history? Because we know we can't discard it? However we answer these questions, the important thing is that the air is now clearer for us to ask them.'

Naysayers will argue that to build a site dedicated to telling the slavery story is being too wedded to the past, but I disagree. To continue to deny lessons from the past is what will keep us tethered to it, stunted from healthy growth. To confidently acknowledge the history, to take ownership of the 'warts and all' narrative (no matter how painful it may be for our modern sensibilities), will be a sign that Bristol is a bold, forward-thinking city, embracing all of the patchwork pieces that make it what it is.

The We Are Bristol History Commission, founded by Mayor Rees after the toppling of the Colston statue, found that people do want to engage meaningfully with the complexities of the city's history and use this to bring people closer together. This led to initiatives such as Spoken Memories, UWE Bristol's partner project, and Bridging Histories, the University of Bristol's project. Both projects have engaged with people across Bristol, finding out what aspects of the city were important in their lives. Regardless of different backgrounds, experiences and social lives, there was a sense of belonging together and a wish to be part of a functioning community in which they could play an active role.

These core shared values on an individual level often get diluted and forgotten in political discourse and policy making, when the majority voice wins through, and it is on such ideals that our sense of modern democracies is founded. This does not (or should not) mean, however, that minority views are meaningless. According to Cornel West (*Race Matters*, 1993), 'Of course, the aim of a constitutional democracy is to safeguard the rights of the minority and avoid the tyranny of the majority.'

A city that ignores the views of its minority voices is one that lacks a full understanding of the needs of its citizens and their frustrations. Bristol needs to avoid this. The conversations about the city and slavery are largely the same as we were having in 2000, in 2007 (the bicentenary of the abolition act) and in 2020, in the aftermath of the statue toppling. Bristol needs to move beyond the cycle of accusations of inaction, face its history and move forward. It is new conversations such as this that the History

Commission have been facilitating.

Although Bath has a confident heritage narrative, it too has problems dealing with its slavery connections. Bath became a famous and wealthy city as the place where merchants and the aristocracy spent their money on leisure and entertainment, the Las Vegas of the South West. The heavy lifting and work went on in Bristol and other port cities, and on the plantations in the Caribbean and Americas. Before Bristol grew prosperous as a port city, Bath was not the wealthy city it eventually became. The two cities have stronger historical ties than either care to admit.

I am fortunate in that I write and have a platform where I can be heard. I try to use these positions to present and discuss some of the views of the people that I know who do not have the same access. I cannot guarantee that people are listening, but I can document these views. As a son of both cities – a child of one and a citizen of the other – I want to be fully seen and heard, as I know we all do. ∎

Shawn-Naphtali Sobers is Professor of Cultural Interdisciplinary Practice at University of the West of England (UWE Bristol). His work includes projects on legacies of slavery in Bristol, Bath, and Nottinghamshire; African presence in Georgian and Victorian Britain; disability and walking; Rastafari language and culture; and creative citizenship in social media. His work has been exhibited and screened nationally and internationally, and he has directed and produced documentaries for BBC, ITV, and Channel 4. Principles relating to community media and participatory practice underpin much of his work. His book, *Black Everyday Lives, Material Culture and Narrative: Tings in de House*, was published in 2023.

> 🔍 Watch *Under the Bridge*, the film made by Shawn Sobers and Rob Mitchell in 2000. How does it resonate with you today?
> http://www.shawnsobers.com/under-the-bridge-film/

"To continue to deny lessons from the past is what will keep us tethered to it, stunted from healthy growth."

1.5

Hollow

Vanessa Kisuule, City Poet 2018-2020

You came down easy in the end.
The righteous wrench of two ropes in a grand plié.

Briefly, you flew, corkscrewed, then met the ground
With the clang of toy guns, loose change, chains, a rain of cheers.

Standing ovation on the platform of your neck.
Punk Ballet. Act 1.
There is more to come.

And who carved you?
They took such care with that stately pose and propped chin.

Wise and virtuous, the plaque assured us.
Victors wish history odourless and static.
But history is a sneaky mistress.

Moves like smoke, Colston,
Like saliva in a hungry mouth.

This is your rightful home,
Here, in the pit of chaos with the rest of us.

Take your twisted glory and feed it to the tadpoles.
Kids will write raps to that syncopated splash.

I think of you lying in the harbour
With the horrors you hosted.
There is no poem more succinct than that.

But still you are permanent.
You who perfected the ratio.
Blood to sugar to money to bricks.

Each bougie building we flaunt haunted by bones.
Children learn and titans sing
Under the stubborn rust of your name.

But the air is gently throbbing with newness.
Can you feel it?

Colston, I can't get the sound of you from my head.
Countless times I passed that plinth,
Its heavy threat of metal and marble.

But as you landed, a piece of you fell off, broke away,
And inside, nothing but air.
This whole time, you were hollow

2

CITY VISIONS

2.1

Can Bristol Take Control of Its Destiny Without Becoming Insular and Elitist?

Julian Baggini

Aristotle argued that the human being is a political animal. We are naturally social beings, and so just as naturally 'when several villages are united in a single complete community, large enough to be nearly or quite self-sufficing, the state comes into existence.' For Aristotle, the stateless individual is like an 'isolated chess piece', what Homer called 'Tribeless, lawless, heartless'.

However, though it is natural to form ourselves into civic units, what form they take and how they are governed is a matter of human artifice. There is no single political model all humanity has adopted. Humans have lived in tribes, fiefdoms, federations, kingdoms, empires, communes, republics and more.

In recent decades, the city has re-emerged as a preferred key unit of political organisation. As the borders of countries have tended towards greater openness and national governments have come to be seen as more and more remote, calls for devolution have grown louder. In the UK, this has centred mainly on the constitutive nations of the United Kingdom. But regions have also been mooted as new centres of power, as have cities and their suburbs. Attempts to establish metro mayors have had mixed results but not so long ago few would even have taken the idea seriously.

One vision of a future Bristol seizes on the potential for it to become a more autonomous city region. Bristol has for a long time prided itself on its independent spirit, championing the local against the might of the national and multinational. The opening of a Tesco Metro store on the street with reportedly the highest proportion of independent businesses in the country was enough to provoke a riot. The experiment with a local currency – the Bristol Pound – ultimately failed but again testifies to the desire for more local self-determination.

One inspiration for this is Preston in Lancashire, which promotes 'Community Wealth Building' by measures such as increasing local procurement and supporting local employers. The 'Preston Model' has been judged a success by many, but the Bristol Pound story is a cautionary tale about the right lessons to learn. It was born of a laudable desire to encourage wealth to stay within the city and to prevent profits being creamed off by national and multinational companies and institutions. Its main practical problem was that it added another layer to financial transactions that made them more expensive to administer. If keeping money local requires spending more of it, then the benefits to locals are questionable.

At a more philosophical level, the idea of drawing a ring around the city's wealth seems misguided. It's the opposite of shutting the gate after the horse has bolted: more like raising the drawbridge once all the horses have been rounded up inside. Whereas Preston was a struggling post-industrial town with good reason to keep and generate more wealth for itself, Bristol is a thriving city which is and has sucked in wealth from outside, through its trade, both legitimate and exploitative. Tobacco helped build the city and in more recent years the international appeal of its creative, aerospace and other industries has put the city on the map. The BBC's Natural History Unit, Aardman Animations and Airbus, for example, are Bristol success stories because they sell around the world in dollars and euros, not Bristol Pounds.

Similarly, many of Bristol's best ethical businesses are ethical precisely because they trade fairly with people from far away. Our many excellent coffee roasters buy their beans from farmers in the Americas, Africa, even India and China. Our first bean-to-bar chocolate maker doesn't source its cacao from Cotham.

Closer to home, there is also a risk that the focus on the city creates an artificial and pernicious divide between Bristol and the wider South West region. Think of all the cafés and restaurants that pride themselves on their local sourcing. Almost all of this comes from further afield than the Metro Mayor's turf: Bristol, South Gloucestershire, Bath and North East Somerset. Without food from Somerset, Devon, Gloucestershire, Wiltshire and South Wales a locavore diet would be severely limited. I am a big fan of the cheese Wandering Ewe, made in Failand, but the producers can barely keep up with demand from local cheese lovers, let alone feed the whole city. There is a growing interest in urban farming, but it is not a credible path to self-sufficiency in the foreseeable future.

Just as the city is dependent on the wider region, so the wider region is dependent on the city. Many come here to work, play, study or for medical care. We are interdependent, from the neighbourhoods to the global level.

But these are not always symmetrical relationships. The coffee farmers who are dependent on artisan cafés and their customers earn a good deal less than both. And the professional middle-classes, more numerous in cities, typically earn more than the rural farmers and cheesemakers whose fare they happily enjoy. Rocketing property prices mean that the less well-off are increasingly priced out of the city, turning into lower-paid service workers living in dormitory towns. The worry is that an increasingly confident, affluent and independent city would be parasitic on the poorer elsewheres that service it. Autonomy is far from noble when it in effect means a power-grab by the already better off.

As well as an economic divide, there is also a growing cultural one. As recent elections and the Brexit referendum showed, the country is increasingly polarised between urban, on average more educated, mobile, cosmopolitan liberals, and the on average more settled, less educated, conservative dwellers of smaller towns and villages. David Goodhart called these two tribes 'anywheres' and 'somewheres' respectively. In my book about the philosophy of the English, *Welcome to Everytown,* I called them liberal cosmopolitans and conservative communitarians. If being Bristolian becomes a stronger identity, associated with the 'anywhere' values of liberal cosmopolitanism, this cultural divide could deepen, further fracturing our already fissiparous nation. It is very easy for pride in our inclusive values to bring with it condescending disdain for those who don't share them.

Is there a way for Bristol to take more control of its own destiny without becoming more narrow, insular and elitist? It's a question that could be asked of any would-be city-state. It requires an answer because without one the risk is that a more autonomous future will be unsustainable and unjust.

A 'People's Republic of Bristol' could thrive if it had justice built into its constitution. Some such binding document would probably be necessary to avoid the city's future charting an ever-changing and inconstant course due to changes in political leadership.

First, it would have to guarantee basic rights to its citizens in ways that the British state has failed to do. Minimum wages would remain a matter of national policy, but they do not provide a living wage in a thriving metropolis. To make life good for all, Bristol would have to make several public service commitments. For example, taking as its model cities like Vienna, it could massively increase its social housing provision to ensure that everyone had a decent home and was not either priced out altogether or 'priced in' to pokey, poor-quality dwellings. Add to this good public services, transport, leisure centres, libraries and parks and Bristol could avoid becoming a rich person's playground serviced by a marginalised poor.

Second, it should guarantee a fair deal for those it trades with. Around the world there are hundreds of Fairtrade cities (including Bristol), villages, zones, boroughs, counties and universities committed to the promotion of Fairtrade certified goods. Since only a few product categories are certified and there are many more ways of trading fairly than are covered by the scheme, there is a pretty low bar for joining. However, it could serve as a prototype for a more ambitious commitment to offer a fair deal for everyone who supplies the city with what it cannot itself produce. Obviously, any local government would be limited in how far it could go down this road and could not control the private purchasing decisions of Bristolians. But by itself adhering to certain standards and certifying businesses that do the same, it could go a long way to making the prosperity of Bristol good for everyone that deals with it.

Third, as part of the United Kingdom, the price of greater autonomy should be a redistribution of some of any extra wealth Bristol earned. To a certain extent this already happens because of central government taxation: richer areas subsidise poorer ones. But this redistribution is uneven. Most notably, the government spends £550 more per head per year in London than it does in the rest of England. Bristol would owe it to the rest of the nation to ensure that more autonomy does not stop it contributing its share to 'levelling up' the whole nation.

How politically viable is such a set of commitments? If the desire for more autonomy is driven by nothing more than the wish to keep more of our money, then the answer is: not very. But I don't think that is what motivates most supporters of greater independence. They want Bristol to be a good global citizen, not a haven for the privileged. To the extent that people seek self-interest, the basic service guarantee should provide more than enough reassurance.

Greater city-based devolution would be unprecedented in the UK and would require political innovation. Any plans for Bristol to lead the way need vision and imagination, both to make plans practical and inspire Bristolians to embrace this untested future. It could be done. The key question is whether it should. ∎

Julian Baggini (JulianBaggini.com) is the author of over 20 books including *Welcome to Everytown: A Journey into the English Mind* and *How to Think Like a Philosopher*. He has served as Academic Director of the Royal Institute of Philosophy and is an Honorary Research Fellow at the University of Kent.

Q Find out more about the Preston model. Do you think it would work in Bristol? https://www.preston.gov.uk/communitywealthbuilding

"A 'People's Republic of Bristol' could thrive if it had justice built into its constitution."

2.2

My Ambitions for Bristol

George Ferguson

Bristol – European Liveable City 2040

'President Caroline Lucas yesterday announced that Bristol has been awarded the accolade of the EU's Most Liveable City, 25 years after it became European Green Capital. She congratulated Bristol and Bath City Region's independent Metro Mayor Professor Alice Roberts for the vision and determination that had brought the city region level with its Danish and Dutch counterparts.'

Dream on!

I was first elected to Bristol City Council 50 years ago in May 1973, having campaigned to save swathes of terrace houses, public green space and the city docks from destruction by massive highway plans that would have torn through many of our historic communities. I had the privilege and experience of representing Cabot Ward in the heart of the city for six years, the best education in real life anyone could have, before resigning from local politics to make a career in architecture and placemaking.

I had arrived in this extraordinary city as a wide-eyed 18-year-old, having lived in various parts of the UK and abroad as my dad was in the military. I came to attend the University of Bristol architecture school, across the road from where I now live in the city centre. I have since travelled the world, learning from wherever I go, but have not moved far.

When I arrived in this 'city of villages' it immediately felt like home and I have had no desire to leave. In 1965 Bristol still seemed to be recovering from the Second World War, with hosts of untended bombsites and derelict buildings overgrown with buddleia, or 'blitz weed', as Bristolians fondly called it.

However, the post-war mindset seemed to have a penchant for vacating and flattening old streets and terraces, to be replaced by soulless blocks set in grass and tarmac. To me, as a naïve young architecture student, it appeared that my wonderful adopted historic city was sacrificing its sense of history and community to the great god car.

A healthy, caring city

I put health at the heart of my vision for Bristol, in an attempt to close that shameful gap of some ten years or more in life expectancy, depending on where you live. To achieve this, we need to make a thousand small moves and just two or three major strategic ones. Most of those small moves will come not from City Hall but, as they always have done, from brilliant individuals and groups within the city who only need to be given permission, and sometimes the means, to bring them to realisation.

Fifteen-minute communities

I referred to Bristol as being 'a city of villages'. Historically that is what we are, with over 100 villages making up one city, making us very different from the 'big boned' metropolitan manufacturing cities such as Birmingham or Manchester. They are great cities but the biggest mistake we make is to emulate their US-style buildings and highways. The wiser thing to do is to reinforce local identity and character, and seek to create a network of '15-minute' healthy communities with all life's needs within easy walking or wheelchair reach. Many of these neighbourhoods would benefit greatly from higher density living to provide the accommodation that is so desperately needed and attract the facilities we all seek. This does not mean encouraging environmentally damaging taller buildings but traditional terraced streets and squares which have proved to provide the best form of medium-rise high-density urban living throughout Europe.

Green city

We should build on the success of our term as the UK's only European Green Capital (2015) to make us the outstanding city of nature and green infrastructure, protecting and fostering our parks and open spaces and linking them all via green, car-free walking and cycling routes. I would fully adopt the 'Car Free Bristol' proposals of the charity Possible, who identify that those currently hit the hardest are 'older people, Disabled people, children and communities where people of colour and poorer people live'.

Healthy schools

I see us becoming a 'city within a forest', trees largely planted by our children through an expansion of our One Tree Per Child initiative, started in 2014.

All schools, primary and secondary, will be rated by their health and environmental credentials and be an integral part of the communities they serve. They will be open outside school hours and during holidays to people of all ages and abilities for everything from further education and volunteering, to care for the elderly and Disabled people. The green road network will be planned on the basis of a combination of safe routes to every school and sanctuaries for wildlife, forming a biodiverse 'web' across the city and beyond. There will be dynamic outside playgrounds and classrooms.

Local food growing

The majority of the city's fresh food will come from the surrounding area via a compact with local farmers freed from the stranglehold of the supermarket chains. The Grade I listed Corn Exchange will be restored as an abundant, continental-style central food market packed with stalls from local farms and makers. This local food culture will be reinforced by vertical farms within the city, making use of defunct multi-storey car parks and all spare roof space.

The listed 'A-Bond' warehouse at Cumberland Basin, which has proved too impractical and expensive to turn into affordable housing, will be a demonstration 'aeroponic' farming project run by Bristol pioneering company LettUs Grow. The 12-acre historic Bristol Zoo site, snatched from the jaws of developers in a last-minute act of generosity, will be a biodiverse walled market garden and food research establishment together with the world's first 'OurWorld Bristol' augmented reality natural world visitor attraction.

Zero Emission Zone

The whole of Bristol will have become a Zero Emission Zone with a maximum 20mph speed limit and zero-emission vehicles only if the city is to meet its zero-carbon target. Every child should be entitled to an upbringing that is as clean and healthy as they would enjoy living in the country, thereby greatly improving quality of life and health for all.

We should aim to make active travel the preferred means of transport within the city by all those who can, with ease of use and priority for disability vehicles by all others, supplemented by light trams and guided buses. Commuting by car into the city during peak hours will be banned following the expansion of park and ride provision and a city region-owned public transport network, including light trams, elevated transit and/or cable cars. These will be clean, comfortable and flexible, gaining huge passenger numbers from those who have decided it is easier to move around the city without a car.

Water and energy

The city region's cleaned-up rivers, canals and docks will be fit for fish, and wild swimmers. A new flood barrier and local crossing at Avonmouth will turn the River Avon and New Cut, down from the M5 bridge, into an anglers' paradise and enable the closing of the Portway to traffic. A traffic-free, nature-rich Avon Gorge will return to its natural state and become a place of learning and leisure on water and land.

The city's district heat network, powered by renewables, will cover the whole city, having learned from Copenhagen, our fellow EU Green Capital and model northern European city. The River Frome will be opened up through the centre and under the M32 as a leisure water park. The M32 will itself be primarily for public and park and ride transport, freeing one side to active travel and to form a new park like New York's High Line, built on an old elevated freight train track in Manhattan.

Connected city

There will be high-speed train connections to London, Birmingham and the North, more essential than ever now that GB air travel will have been restricted by Parliament to islands and the more remote areas of an independent Scotland. The majority of Bristol Airport parking will have been returned to agriculture.

There is so much more that could be said on many more issues, but I hope this gives a flavour of my dream for a healthy, caring and connected Bristol.

I still stand by the vision for Bristol I published ten years ago, available on peopleandcities.com. Much has flowed under the bridge since then but the needs and aspirations are little changed. We can't afford to wait another ten years. ■

George Ferguson was President of the Royal Institute of British Architects (RIBA) 2003-2005 and the directly elected mayor of Bristol 2012-2016. His work can be seen at peopleandcities.com

---

🔍 Read about the Car Free Cities campaign. What would be needed for Bristol to be car free? https://www.wearepossible.org/carfreecities

---

"I had arrived in this extraordinary city as a wide-eyed 18-year-old, having lived in various parts of the UK and abroad... I have since travelled the world, learning from wherever I go, but have not moved far."

2.3

Why Cities Need Feminism

Sian Norris

This essay, I'm sorry to say, starts with a murder.

In December 2010, the student Joanna Yeates was killed in Bristol. As the police hunted for her killer, the city's women were put under a familiar sort of lockdown. We were warned not to walk home alone after dark, despite the fact it got dark at 4pm. We were urged to get taxis rather than risk walking or taking public transport, despite the fact that a year before, a cab driver was revealed to have been one of Britain's most prolific rapists; despite the fact that cabs are expensive and women are, on average, poorer than men. The message for the city's women was clear. Stay home. Don't walk alone. Be safe.

The unspoken coda to such a message is always there. The threat that if you don't follow the rules, then we can't be blamed for what happens to you. Don't follow the rules, and it's your fault.

Men, on the other hand, were free from such warnings. They could go about their business. Walk in the dark. Get drunk before Christmas. Keep going. Don't worry. Don't stop.

Yeates' killer was eventually arrested. He was her neighbour. He had attacked a woman before. With him in custody, women were free to walk the streets again, free to stay out after 4pm. But the messages we heard in that time, which were the same messages we have heard since we were very young, they never truly leave us. We never truly feel free. We never really get to believe the city is for us.

***

The reason I start with a murder is because what happened next in Bristol proves the point of this essay. That point is: cities need feminists.

Not long after Yeates' horrific death, Bristol changed the way it ran women's safety campaigns. Gone were the dire warnings that restricted women's freedoms. The stern faces and wagging fingers, which told women it was our fault if we were assaulted, raped or killed, were packed away. Instead, the city launched a campaign telling men what consent looks like. The posters warned men that a short skirt didn't mean she was asking for it. Slogans targeted perpetrators of domestic abuse and sought to shame them for their behaviour.

The new safety campaign came after a huge upsurge of feminist activity in Bristol. I was part of it. I had thrown myself into feminism with a fury borne of never feeling fully free. Bristol Fawcett was lobbying for political and structural change, while the Bristol Feminist Network was making lots of noise with Reclaim the Night marches outside City Hall. Together the feminist groups worked to raise awareness of men's violence against women, women's safety, victim-blaming culture and how the sexual objectification of women allowed for men's violence to be normalised and accepted. Sometimes we worked in partnership, sometimes we worked side-by-side, sometimes we worked apart. But we were always together, united in our demands for a fairer, more equal Bristol, a better world. Through formal political campaigning and rabble-rousing, petitions, appeals, cabaret nights, consciousness-raising, marches, council submissions, meetings, guerrilla campaigns and more, feminist activism was stamped all over our city.

Such energy was nothing new to Bristol. As we took our Reclaim the Night march from City Hall, through Broadmead and down Stokes Croft to Portland Square, we were standing on the shoulders of feminist giants.

***

Did you know there's a blue plaque in Bristol for the suffragette Annie Kenney? The militant feminist hailed from the trade union tradition, a working-class fighter for justice who came to Bristol in 1907 to set up the Women's Social and Political Union's (WSPU) West of England branch, creating a thriving and politically voracious activist scene in one of the UK's most radical cities.

All too often, the popularly understood history of women's rights focuses on one or two key names, one or two 'hubs'. In the suffragette movement, that name is Pankhurst, and the hubs are London and Manchester. The names of women like Kenney, and the activism in cities such as Bristol, can get lost in a hero narrative.

This is, in fact, a patriarchal way of exploring history – one that relies on the Great Man narrative, but with the Man swapped in for an Exceptional Woman. This loses how history is made up of movements, of people coming together to create change. It is not driven by individuals but by collective action. And while there may be leaders or organisers, they are not solely responsible for bringing about change. Taking a more feminist approach to history allows us to see that the rights we have won in Bristol today came not from the Exceptional Woman of History, but from collaboration and movement-building.

Miles from Manchester and London, Bristol had a thriving and active suffrage movement. Theresa Garnett was arrested for confronting Churchill when he arrived at Bristol Temple Meads. Mary Sophia Allen went to Horfield Gaol after smashing windows at the Board of Trade Office. Lillian Mary-Dove Wilcox, born in Bedminster, Bristol, and a member of the West of England WSPU, was not as peaceful as her name suggested: a member of Emmeline Pankhurst's guard, she travelled around the UK demanding votes for women, getting arrested in Glasgow. Vera Holme and Elsie Howey hid in the Colston Hall organ, interrupting a cabinet meeting by bursting out and shouting 'votes for women'.

The skills of direct action and the realisation that women could and should demand political change meant the drive and energy of these women did not start and end with the right to vote. Many of Bristol's feminist fighters had, like Annie Kenney, a political background in the trade union movement. Jessie Stephen, who organised girls working as maids as well as being part of the WSPU, became a Bristol councillor who fought for women's right to birth control. Feminist activism in Bristol has always been about recognising that the fight for rights is bigger than one battle. While the battle for the vote gave women political status, the women fighting that battle knew we could not be free if we were exploited in the workplace or denied bodily integrity.

***

Decades after the suffragettes leapt out of Colston Hall's organ, Bristol was on the forefront of second wave feminist activism to tackle men's violence against women. Two anti-rape groups formed in the city: the first was the Women's Centre, and a second was aligned to the Wages for Housework campaign. Feminists in the city linked up with women's rights organisations across the country, rallying Reclaim the Night marches and providing safe havens for survivors of men's violence. It was that legacy of the women's liberation movement that birthed the feminist movement of the late 2000s and early 2010s, when women like me danced on the city streets with our second-wave sisters, as we continued to demand our safety and our freedom.

***

Bristol's rich feminist history has led to a feminist present. The determined campaigning of women across the ages has helped to put women's rights at the heart of formal political activity in the city: we are the only council to have a cabinet member for women and children, and all but one of our four MPs are women. Women have attained the positions of leadership dreamed of by the suffragettes. Far from having to hide in a musical instrument, a woman is now in charge of the newly named Bristol Beacon (formerly Colston Hall).

But challenges remain. The rate of domestic abuse in Bristol is 29.2 per 1,000 people, with women nearly three times more likely to be victims than men. The city's deep-rooted inequalities mean that women in Hartcliffe and Withywood are far more likely to be victims of gender-based violence than their peers in wealthier areas.

How do we overcome those challenges? How do we build a feminist future for Bristol? The answer is the same as it was in 1909, 1971, 2007: by feminist organising. It was feminist organising that helped bring suffragettes into Bristol's council where they advocated for birth control and human rights. It was feminist organising in the second wave that opened refuges and changed the conversation about rape and men's violence. And it was feminist organising in the twenty-first century that helped to tackle harmful myths and stereotypes that made women and girls less safe, including in the fight against female genital mutilation.

Whenever the word feminism is mentioned, there is opposition. But by building on that feminist heritage and harnessing more than a century of ferocious feminist energy we can build a better Bristol, one where women have equal access to public space, and equal access to political space. It'll be a Bristol where care is valued, and where boys are raised to respect their sisters, and where the toxic combination of regional and gendered inequality is gone, making a healthier and happier city for every citizen.

Annie Kenney described the fight for the vote as follows: 'The work was hard, we did it. Opposition fierce: we overcame it. Dangers were many: we faced them. And in the end we won.'

We haven't won yet. But we can win a better Bristol if we put feminism at its heart. ■

Sian Norris is a writer and investigative journalist who has covered far-right movements and their relocation to the mainstream for a range of publications, including the UK's *Times* newspaper and *The Observer*. She is the author of *Bodies Under Siege: How the Far-Right Attack on Reproductive Rights Went Global*. In 2012 she set up the Bristol Women's Literature Festival, which she ran for eight years.

> Q Discover the Feminst Archives and explore the rich history of collective action in the city https://feministarchivesouth.org.uk/. Consider joining a collective, such as Bristol Women's Voice https://www.bristolwomensvoice.org.uk/

"Bristol's rich feminist history has led to a feminist present."

2.4

How Do We Build a City of Aspiration?

Poku Osei

Just as for countless individuals who came before me, Bristol has become my cherished home. This city stands as a beacon of economic prowess in the United Kingdom, ranking among the top 20 local economies in terms of gross value added growth in 2022.

Bristol is renowned as one of the finest places to reside in the UK, celebrated for its financial strength and forward-thinking nature. It is a haven of culture and innovation. However, if we delve beneath the surface of affluence and liberalism, we uncover a distressing reality. Among the 348 districts across England and Wales, Bristol ranks as the seventh most challenging place for ethnic minorities to live and thrive.

Inequality permeates our city, concealing a disheartening undercurrent of marginalisation, limited social mobility and deprivation that disproportionately affects ethnic minority communities. The outlook appears bleak unless we take coordinated action. Bristol finds itself grappling with the reverberations of the Covid-19 pandemic, recent geopolitical and macroeconomic shifts and a cost-of-living crisis. These challenges weigh heavily on ethnic minorities in our city, exacerbating their struggles.

Furthermore, the introduction of artificial intelligence and climate technology compounds the challenge as traditional education systems (state schools) face difficulties in preparing students for the swiftly changing demands of the workforce. This is a particular problem for inner-city state schools, where over 65 per cent of ethnic minority children are educated.

Consequently, we face a future where far too many ethnic minorities of working age experience unemployment, underemployment or a decline in real wages. This engenders despondency, leading too many brilliant minds toward lives of crime and squandering the immense talent that underpins our city's potential to compete in an increasingly globalised market. Ultimately, it jeopardises the cultural richness, economic prosperity and social harmony that Bristol has enjoyed in recent years.

The questions we must confront are: What can we do to address this pressing issue? How can we safeguard the next generation of ethnic minorities from entrenched inequality and limited social mobility? How can we break the cycle of deprivation and dependency on welfare for aspiring ethnic minorities and young people from low-income backgrounds?

We must acknowledge that supporting our youth in pursuing their professional aspirations requires more than linear talent development. It necessitates a multidimensional approach that takes into account institutional practices, employer biases and discriminatory policies.

In response to these challenges, Babbasa, the award-winning social enterprise based in Bristol that I founded, advocates for our city to commit to a bold, long-term goal for the betterment of our ethnic minority children and young people. A goal that could ignite creativity among our city leaders, foster collaboration among practitioners and policymakers, and inspire citizens to actively pursue equal opportunities and inclusion.

In 2022, Babbasa conducted a survey of over 1,000 young people and held 28 consultations with Bristol's businesses, educational institutions, communities and public organisations, in partnership with Arup and the University of Bristol. These efforts culminated in the Socio-Economic Analysis Report of 2022, which benchmarked the extent and scale of our city's inequality gap and indicated what such a long-term goal could look like.

In 2023, Babbasa joined forces with key city partners, including Bristol City Council, Cabot Learning Federation, Black South West Network (BSWN), the University of the West of England (UWE Bristol), University of Bristol, ARUP, Business West and the mayor of Bristol, to make two significant announcements. First, the city's adoption of a visionary long-term goal to support at least one young person from each low-income household, beginning in inner-city Bristol, to secure a role with a median salary by 2030. Second, a commitment from the key city partners to support an evidence-based and groundbreaking programme of work to realise this long-term goal.

This visionary goal and programme of work, known as OurCity2030, seeks to unlock the untapped potential of Bristol's ethnic minority population. It aspires to nurture the next generation of coders, creatives, activists, architects, engineers, entrepreneurs and social scientists, representing diverse backgrounds in terms of race, faith, culture and class.

On an individual level, the OurCity2030 plan aims to lift 2,030 ethnic minority young people into meaningful careers by 2030, thereby improving workplace representation and enhancing the earning potential of ethnic minorities in the city. Over time, it seeks to close the inequality gap by increasing the percentage of ethnic minorities in career-oriented, leadership and management positions, and foster a new generation of economically successful ethnic minority role models for young people from low-income households to admire and emulate.

At the city level, the projected positive effects of OurCity2030 will include increased student loan repayments, local tax revenue and greater access to mortgages, as more ethnic minorities secure stable employment opportunities. The enhanced workforce representation is also expected to contribute to advancements in innovation and profitability for companies, thanks to the diversity of thought that will emerge.

On the national stage, we expect the OurCity2030 programme to ignite purposeful cross-sector collaborations, research partnerships, and a replicable social mobility model. We plan to share the OurCity2030 model and lessons learnt with other cities along the way, so that they too can implement the multidimensional programme to positively affect equal access to employment opportunities, employer behaviours and structural policy changes that lead us towards a fairer, more equitable and inclusive society.

Together, I believe we can shape a brighter future for Bristol – one where equality, opportunity and inclusion thrive. I'm therefore urging all to rally around OurCity2030, a vision that embodies the best of what our city has to offer and sets a course for lasting transformation. ■

Poku Osei is an award-winning social entrepreneur with a passion for levelling the playing field for low income and ethnic minority groups. He is the founder and CEO of Babbasa, the first Black-led social enterprise to win the prestigious Queen's Award for Enterprise (Social Mobility) in 2020, for transforming the lives of over 2,200 ethnic minority young people in the UK. He is also the co-founder of the Black Professionals Network and Founding Curator of the World Economic Forum initiative – Bristol Global Shapers Hub.

Q Join the Our City 2030 movement https://www.ourcity2030.com/

"OurCity2030 aims to lift 2,030 ethnic minority young people into meaningful careers by 2030…"

How Do We Work Together to Build Philanthropy for a Future City?

Suzanne Rolt

The Ancient Greeks have taught us a great many things, passing on knowledge and values as relevant today as they were some 2,500 years ago. Language is one of their most enduring legacies, still evident in the alphabetic symbols that denote the workings of mathematical and scientific thought, and in the roots of words that form the basis of so many of our own. One such word is philanthropy, which we commonly use to describe the transference of wealth to charitable causes. In the Greek it derives from 'philos', meaning loving, in the sense of caring for or nourishing, and 'anthropos', meaning human being. In combination, they speak to a 'love of humankind', a concept that goes beyond the act of helping others, expressing something altogether more profound: the motivation and purity of purpose that lies behind it.

Over time, the meaning of philanthropy has narrowed, becoming associated less with a selfless and civic-minded sharing of time, skills and care, and more with very public displays of wealth made by the powerful and privileged. Bristol's history over the past 650 years has been populated by many such figures, people who profited from the city's status as a major trading port, accumulating wealth on an almost unimaginable scale. They made fortunes through the trade of wine and timber, sugar, tobacco and, for a period we look back on with shame, enslaved people. It was often these same fortunes that provided the means to bestow substantial gifts on charitable and civic institutions and projects, contributing to the growing prosperity and culture of Bristol.

The philanthropy that built and shaped so much of Bristol remains highly visible today. It is enshrined in the architecture of its great civic set pieces, its cathedrals, churches, schools and universities. It resides in council chambers, in the names of the 'great and good' chiselled into the stone walls, and amongst the exhibits in museums and galleries. Most controversially, it is recorded on monuments and statues, erected in the full expectation that they would stand in perpetuity. The personal motivations and legacies of individual philanthropists are complex, and the majority of philanthropic gifts in our area are entirely unconnected with these historic trades. The world, and Bristol with it, has changed greatly over the past centuries, and so too has the nature and role of philanthropy.

While Bristol regularly tops the lists of the most desirable places to live, there is growing recognition of its status as a city of two halves. The students who arrive each year to study, often staying on to live and work here, are joined by thousands more relocating in pursuit of well-remunerated jobs in finance, engineering and the technology and creative industries. But alongside them live many more again who find that these same opportunities for progression elude them. Subsistence is often the height of attainment and even this is threatened by exceptional events such as the Covid-19 pandemic, the cost-of-living crisis, or the longer-term challenges of climate change. This divide is clearly illustrated by the growth in private wealth: the richest one per cent of people in the UK are now wealthier than 70 per cent of the population combined, according to Oxfam in January 2023.

Into this picture comes inherited wealth, which remains attached to the few, further distorting an already unequal terrain. Over the next 20 to 30 years, the biggest ever transfer of inherited wealth in UK history is set to take place. Baby Boomers will pass £5.5 trillion of inheritance and gifts down to Millennials. Will this contribute to the widening of existing inequalities, or could it be an opportunity to address this inequality through wider engagement in new thinking and solutions?

In recent times, people have carried inherited wealth more heavily, conscious of their place in a system that has disadvantaged and disenfranchised so many. Their own children may not yet think of themselves as the philanthropists of the future – certainly the named plaque on a building holds little attraction for this younger generation – but reports suggest that they are socially conscious and aware of the responsibilities they have to communities around them. We see, too, how rapidly younger donors mobilise to support causes they believe in, sharing them on social media and crowdfunding platforms.

Future philanthropy trends are of prime concern at the organisation I run, Quartet Community Foundation, a Bristol-based grant-making charity that works across the West of England. Quartet is part of a worldwide movement of community foundations that began in 1914 in America and now has nearly 2,600 members, including 47 across the UK. What connects each one is a commitment to meeting the long-term, changing needs of local communities through the championing of local philanthropy, principally through the building of a permanent fund known as an endowment. This model balances the traditional view of philanthropy as being only centred around an individual's wishes with a more collective endeavour: individuals, groups and businesses who share a sense of common purpose aligning their efforts to affect positive change. Community foundations work in partnership with local authorities and can be a channel for funding from national and devolved structures, but the key point is that they remain independent, making them a trusted partner at grassroots level.

The success of this approach over time means that some American foundations have grown billion-dollar endowments. Drawing on substantial annual investment returns, they can act strategically, addressing not only the symptoms but also the underlying causes of systemic, entrenched inequality. Established later than the American foundations, we are some way behind in the UK, but Quartet is one of the country's largest. It has given out nearly £70 million to local charities and voluntary sector groups since 1986, including £6 million in grants in the past year. We have close to 400 fund holders, deeply committed individuals and organisations who choose to donate large parts of their wealth. They direct their giving through Quartet, supporting organisations working across virtually every area of need in our region and across all age groups, including housing and homelessness, health and wellbeing, poverty and inequality, and issues arising from climate change. These needs are persistent and even as we seek solutions for existing ones, new ones appear on the horizon. This is the backdrop for our determination to inspire and persuade new generations of private and corporate donors of the value, and necessity, of philanthropy.

So, what role might philanthropy play in the future city? Some would argue that its very existence is a sign of failure, an acknowledgement that the state cannot provide the essentials of a good life for all its citizens. Or that philanthropy could be said to be a product of the wealth systems that create these very inequalities in the first place. But with populations rising, the challenges of climate change and resources stretched to breaking point, many others would argue that we need to open up, not close down, options for change. There is huge untapped potential in greater numbers of people and businesses directing their financial resources with intention, helping the city to adapt to future challenges and opportunities.

The organisations that promote philanthropy are themselves embracing change and diversifying and democratising their approach, including their internal structures. This includes embedding racial justice and participatory, citizen-led approaches into grant making, and considering how philanthropy can combine with social investment to fund, say, affordable homes. They are supporting innovation and working with fund holders who are not afraid to take risks and, when necessary, to challenge the status quo. Importantly, they are using evidence and data to identify the needs and priorities in a local area. All this goes far beyond the simple distribution of well-meaning gifts.

More and more of late we have heard the phrase, 'this shouldn't be happening in today's society'. We read of teachers using their own money to buy food, toothbrushes and clothes for children in their classrooms, or families facing the impossible choice between 'eat or heat'. Philanthropy has too often been seen as something that funds the non-essentials, expressing the personal preferences of rich people who are far removed from real life. This portrayal no longer holds true and helps no one. The philanthropy of the now and the future is about identifying priorities, aligning resources and acknowledging that no single sector can act alone in solving the persistent needs of their communities.

I return to the Greek origins of philanthropy and to a way of thinking of, and perceiving, the possibility of a better world. It is not just the love of the people we live and work alongside, but those we pass each day and whose lives we glimpse in the shadow of our own and cannot ignore. From small acts of kindness to gifts of time, skills and money, philanthropy devoid of personal vanity can be a symbol of communal strength and solidarity. We know that the next generation of philanthropists are out there and have the potential to become highly engaged change makers. Together, we have a simple choice to make: what truly, lastingly matters to us? This should be the driving force that shapes our future city. ∎

Suzanne Rolt is Chief Executive of Quartet Community Foundation. She has held a number of executive and non-executive roles in the cultural and charity sectors at both a local and national level. Before joining Quartet, she was CEO of the concert venue St George's Bristol, where she led a transformational capital project.

🔍 Get advice on the best ways to support your local community needs
https://quartetcf.org.uk/help-with-your-giving/for-individuals-families/

"The philanthropy of the now and the future is about identifying priorities, aligning resources and acknowledging that no single sector can act alone in solving the persistent needs of their communities."

2.6

Bristol Bristol

Miles Chambers, City Poet 2016-2018
Rewritten with Steve Duncan

Bristol Bristol the city that was built on the bricks of heroic hardship.
Bristol Bristol the place of dreams and possibilities, the place of creative aspirations,
culture, commerce and its own seductive music

Bristol Bristol a place still haunted by the ancestral ghost that echoes the historical
hangover that yet sobered us up to what time hasn't changed.
Bristol Bristol. Take a walk. Be inspired. Feel the magical connection, see a positive
future. Come dance in this festival of ideas

See, we don't have to wait for carnival every year. The party is right now right here
this very stage, the very atmosphere is encouraging us to lose our fear 'cause
geographically there's no no-go areas round here

Stand on the Suspension Bridge, see the communities within a community integrated
not segregated and in the distance you can almost reach out and grab Glastonbury

Oh city of paradoxes why all this controversy?
Oh conflicting urbanisation I love you but what are you doing to me?

Amidst the beauty I regularly see the women of the street exploiting their femininity.
Being exploited by their calamity

I love you Bristol. I love the clamour of the weekend drinkers and the hustle and the
bustle of the 9-5

I hate you Bristol as I watch every day the young kiddy with the old weathered face in
a Tesco shop doorway clinging to his blanket of security begging to survive.
I love you because of my first kiss from Samantha, because of the smell of Pieminister.

Because of the aroma of Agnes Spencer, because of the pull of colourful air balloons floating aimlessly in a blue sky.

I love you Bristol 'cause of the first play I wrote here, 'cause of the first film we shot here, 'cause of the first poem I performed here and left my inspired listeners with one notion; Just try!

I question the graffiti that glares at you echoing the voices of imprisoned youth. Then I hear a different cheer, the screams of Rovers and City fans on a Saturday morning celebrating a different truth.

I belong here Bristol amongst the riots and the protest,
Amongst the fighting for equality
I belong here Bristol amongst the ranters and the ravers, the Gospel singers, the multicultural students studying effectively
I belong here Bristol with the Bristol blue taxis, the 'cheers drive' shirt and jeans top. Blokes braving the winter streets to look cool
I belong here Bristol with the scantily clad beautified stiletto brigade wearing the same skirts they used to wear to school
I belong here Bristol with the privileged pupils parading their privileged uniforms and the under-privileged not being encouraged to perform
I belong here Bristol. You taught me the special secrets of wild life and movie makers can see the magic in this storm
I belong here Bristol amongst the travellers and the hippies that ask me to think about life in a different way
I belong here Bristol amongst those that visit to work and study and exclaim 'I just gotta stay'.
I belong here Bristol with the 'Old Money' business and the entrepreneurs wheeling, dealing, trying to own this city
I belong here Bristol with all those food-crazed ideas and food-crazed delicious somethings emulating whatshisname; Jamie

I belong here Bristol with the Bristol sound echoing sentiments of who I am flowing through my ears
I belong here with the faith-based streets trying to get you to come to God with all your fears

Oh city of paradoxes where you going to take me today?
Oh conflicting urbanisation are you going to show me a better way?

So what fate awaits this colourful city?
We need to consider every beneficial possibility.
Transport punctuality
Drugs and social policy
Religion ethnicity
Multiculturalism and unity
Economy and prosperity
Education and opportunity
Business and creativity
Media and honesty
Religion and spirituality
Acknowledgement and generosity

I belong here with the good schools offering a good future to a bad past. The bad schools offering a bad future to a good past. It's here on these streets that the youth are spitting the lyrics of the future that will change the wrong decisions of the past. I belong here! Right now in this place we have the opportunity to be something great, something amazing together... To utilise the collective potential of us all. That will make this place unique and special... Let's answer the call. I belong right here!

3

SOCIAL JUSTICE AND BRISTOL

Garden City
Pam Beddard

When the Covid-19 pandemic put an end to the overseas travel that is usually part of everyday life for the Bristol-based wildlife cameraman Martin Dohrn, he turned his lenses instead onto his own city-centre garden.

The resulting film, *My Garden of a Thousand Bees*, provided revelatory insights into how and where bees nest, rest, feed and breed, and it went on to win worldwide acclaim and awards, including an Emmy nomination and the top prize at the international Wildscreen Festival of natural history film and TV.

It also underscored the value of urban gardens not only to the winged insect essential to the production of a third of what humans eat (plus many medicines, fabrics, animal feeds and other useful materials), but to the wellbeing of life as a whole.

This is an especially important point for the future of expanding cities like Bristol, where the drive to create new housing is putting pressure on both greenfield and brownfield sites and where many of the approved or proposed new-builds are for high-density towers or terraces.

In Bristol, as elsewhere, objections greet nearly every application to build new homes, often about the scale, density, design, materials, loss of trees, impact on traffic or vistas, but it's rare to see any that ask, 'where are the gardens?'. It's a question that deserves higher priority if the UK is ever to climb from being the worst country in the G7 bloc of wealthy nations and third worst in all of Europe for biodiversity.

And a climb is both necessary and urgent, because while many cherish wildlife for its own sake, that trilling blackbird, cute fox cub, bluebell carpet, towering oak, slithering earthworm – even the slug – all help to make and keep Planet Earth habitable.

Ignoring the need for improvement isn't an option if future Bristol is to take full advantage of the circa £1.8 trillion-worth of services that nature donates to the UK – as crop pollinators, soil enrichers, water cleaners, pest controllers, noise and pollution absorbers, waste recyclers, flood mitigators, heatwave coolers, anxiety soothers, health doctors, oxygen suppliers and capturers of climate-altering carbon dioxide.

Many amateur gardeners, including allotment holders, are already doing their bit to stem nature losses – losses which mean the UK has so far failed to reach 17 out the 20 biodiversity targets set by the UN ten years ago.

Keepers of the handkerchief-sized plots so common in Bristol's inner city may feel that little difference will be made just because they favour bee, bird and butterfly-friendly native plants over showy exotics; provide food, water and shelter for wildlife; add greenery to the roofs of bike or bin stores and sheds; or leave brambles intact and lawns unmown – but there really is strength in numbers.

After all, it's estimated that across the UK, household gardens make up around 1.8 million acres, the equivalent of five National Parks each as big as Dartmoor, potentially an enormous nature reserve.

Alas, gardens, too, are under threat. Along with the current 'pack 'em in' trend in housing design, factors such as parking pressures and the growth in home e-car charging stations mean increasing amounts of hard-standing are in evidence in front gardens across the city. In addition, inquiries about installing artificial lawns rose by 185 per cent during lockdown, despite much evidence that they deny many useful minibeasts a refuge, add to flood and stormwater overflow risks and very probably leech microplastics into the food chain.

The bigger challenge, however, is with the larger sites.

Bristol wants to build 30,000-plus new homes by 2036. Sites recently or currently eyed for these developments, or already taken over, include some key wildlife habitats: Ashton Meadows, Bristol Zoo, Brislington Meadows, the banks of the Avon, Filwood Park and Novers Hill / Western Slopes.

Bristol planners do expect developers to include some environment-friendly features, but a like-for-like replacement of lost habitat via gardens, green roofs or living facades is rarely demanded. In addition to this, there are often other ways in which house-building aspirations of private developers, or the council's own Goram Homes, conflict to a major degree with the city and the country's biodiversity action plans and ambitions.

Look, for instance, at Yew Tree Farm, Bishopsworth, the last working farm within the city's boundaries, an organic meat and vegetable supplier supposedly part of the Green Belt and a hedgerow, meadow and species-rich Site of Special Nature Conservation Interest. In spring 2023, without forewarning, a contractor working on behalf of an agent for a London-based property company turned up with the intention of slashing a 12-metre hole in the ancient hedgerow bordering a field the farmer leases, apparently believing this would advance the property company's hopes of selling the land to the Redrow building company and building over 200 homes.

The assault on the hedge – a haven for birds, bees, butterflies, small mammals, invertebrates and wildflowers – was stopped, but the threat remains, not least because Bristol City planners earned cross-party condemnation and a mayoral rebuke for failing to respond in time with a firm 'No' to an application to waive The Hedgerow Regulations 1997.

It was a shambles, but hedges aren't alone in being threatened with cuts. Council planning teams are also being scythed at a time when the pace and complexity of planning matters is rising.

The bedrooms vs biodiversity battle threatens to get worse due to Biodiversity Net Gain (BNG) legislation coming into force (November 2023, large sites; April 2024, small sites). The basic idea is sound. Under BNG, developers are expected to improve biodiversity by ten per cent. But there's a get-out clause where this poses on-site difficulties, and several companies are already offering house builders a way to buy BNG 'units' elsewhere. Fine for them but less so for the hedgehog, frog, bumblebee, bat or swift family that's relied on the same spot for generations.

As the Bristol One City Ecological Emergency Action Plan points out, radical change is needed.

How radical, though?

Other councils and countries are providing a steer on what can be done.

Exeter and the Duchy of Cornwall now require the installation of at least one 'bird brick' in every new home. Chickenfeed at circa £50 a go, yet with huge potential to help Red-Listed swifts, house sparrows and house martins to successfully raise chicks. Edinburgh's city hall is roofed with a wildflower meadow. Islington Council is funding 38 projects that will add many more trees, flowerbeds and herb and vegetable plots across the borough.

In Australia, Austria, Denmark and France (to name just a few), it is now mandatory to integrate a green roof into new-builds. In Berlin, Cologne, Munich and Rotterdam, householders can get discounts on water bills when making a property more environmentally friendly helps to ease stormwater run-off. Cities across Canada are signing up to a Municipal Natural Assets Initiative, tackling biodiversity losses and the climate challenge. In New York, greening an apartment block earns a property tax reduction.

Singapore is going even further. It is mainstreaming biodiversity considerations throughout its entire application-to-completion planning process by demanding green roofs, green facades, roadside trees, full protection of on-site habitats and corridors maintaining habitat links. Development must also fit in with ambitious species recovery plans for more than 150 plants and animals and there's an insistence that no home is more than a ten-minute walk from a place of nature.

Adopting similar ideas is one way to help the city deliver on its vision of becoming carbon neutral and climate resilient by 2030. Recruiting gardens and gardeners to the cause would speed action up. Not all steps can be taken immediately; some may even need changes to council tax or planning law. But some quick fixes might be possible:

- A city-wide campaign explaining how and why to become a wildlife-friendly gardener and counselling against the introduction of non-porous surfaces, especially artificial lawns.

- A revision of the council's mowing schedules for hedges, verges and pocket parks so that they respect when native wildflowers are most abundant, and/or No Mow May.
- Free market stall use for non-profits/growers specialising in bird, bee and butterfly-friendly gardening goods, including plants/seeds.
- Free or discounted green waste collections and/or communal bins for existing and new housing areas with a high percentage of bee, bird and butterfly-friendly frontages/ backyards/surroundings.
- A veto on any BNG proposals for offsetting more than a mile from the damaged area.
- Firmer pressure on developers to retain and improve on-site biodiversity.
- The chance for streets/developments to earn a sign advertising that the area is a biodiversity action champion.

New housing is needed, of course, but there's no point in making wildlife homeless to achieve it. It risks Planet Earth no longer being a viable home for any and all living things, including us. ■

Pam Beddard is a writer and publicist based in south Bristol whose work credits include devising and delivering campaigns for the Avon, Somerset and Wiltshire Wildlife Trusts, the Countryside Agency, Forestry Commission England, the Natural History Museum's Wildlife Photographer of the Year competition, the Wildfowl and Wetlands Trust, Whitley Fund for Nature, the Woodland Trust and several overseas-based wildlife conservation NGOs.

Q Visit Grow Wilder and take one of their green-fingered courses for inspiration on wilding your garden https://www.avonwildlifetrust.org.uk/explore/grow-wilder

"As the Bristol One City Ecological Emergency Action Plan points out, radical change is needed."

3.2

What Could a Universal Basic Income Deliver in a Future Bristol?

Geoff Crocker

In the city of the future, citizens would feel secure and able to flourish. That includes income security. Technology is both forcing and enabling lifestyle change. The best response is to maximise the gains it offers and mediate any loss it imposes. Automation will continue to offer a plethora of accessible services, but will also continue to change employment patterns, and the income which goes with employment. Some jobs will be lost; other new services will create jobs. Retraining may become regular in a flexible job market. The gig economy may flourish, for some a fulfilling lifestyle, but creating precarious income. Even if total employment holds up, evidence suggests that total employment income across the city may decline as technology sucks labour income out of the economy. For some citizens, household income may become inadequate, meaning that for the city economy, demand will decline. We already suffer the phenomenon of in-work poverty, meaning that full employment work and wages no longer guarantee adequate household income.

Citizens of this future technology-intensive city will need a basic income for their financial security. The basic income proposal is for all citizens to receive a regular money income into their bank account unconditionally. Citizens currently receive a basic income, but from a mixture of work, welfare benefits and pensions. This pattern will continue to change. Inadequate working income means that too often families have to resort to increased household debt. Meanwhile, welfare benefits remain targeted and therefore highly conditional. Conditionality too easily becomes harsh and severe, intrusive and humiliating. Take-up is often low, especially in vulnerable groups like the elderly. And, most importantly, conditionality creates unemployment and poverty traps, because benefits are withdrawn if people take work, therefore acting as a disincentive. Until recently, anyone receiving benefit effectively lost 96 per cent of income from new work. Universal Credit has reduced this to 70 per cent, but the taper is still disincentivising. Basic income suffers no withdrawal if someone takes work.

An ideal city of the future would not be characterised as a community with inadequate or precarious income, increased household debt and a harsh conditional welfare system. The security of an unconditional basic income would increase individual and family wellbeing, as well as increasing social cohesion through a strengthened sense of belonging. Indeed, basic income is a human right. We all have a shared and equal right to the infrastructure of the city we inherit, and to the inherited technology which fires its productive economy. This citizen's birth right is expressed in a universal basic income. Basic income addresses the social injustice of inequality of today's city.

The common objection to basic income is that it is either too small to be meaningful, or too large to be affordable. I've addressed this question of affordability, both on the website 'The Case for Basic Income' at www.ubi.org and in my book *Basic Income and Sovereign Money*. I've also pointed out that the Covid-19 pandemic generated a huge macroeconomic pilot of basic income. In the furlough scheme, we paid £24,000/year to three million people, costing a total of £69 billion, all of which was funded as part of the Bank of England's purchase of £875 billion of government debt, essentially directly funding government expenditure by debt-free money creation. It worked OK.

Here, I'd like to focus more on the effect of universal unconditional basic income on the community of the city of the future. For most of us, full-time work has meant a five-day week, working 8am to 4pm in a factory, 9am to 5pm in an office, or retail hours in a shop. This fixed structure has started to change. Many people now work part-time, or partly from home. Technology may mean that we all need to work less. This gives us an opportunity to rethink, to reconceptualise our lives. Working hours per week have declined consistently over the last several decades. Perhaps we will be able to work a 15-hour week as Keynes predicted so long ago? Philosophically, we may become less work-centric, less defined by our work and more by our creative potential. Do we fear 'having more time on our hands', or can we flourish in the context of this new opportunity? Work is important for things other than income, including social networking and interaction, personal dignity and a sense of belonging. So how can the culture of the future city adapt and evolve to support new lifestyles?

Perhaps we can consider the experience of people who have retired from work for some answers. Very few of them are desperate to return to work, just as many people currently at work aren't anxious to work more but are keen to get home at the end of their working day. Options for increased leisure, creative activity and engagement abound. Once free from the income requirements of commercial market work, all sorts of non-market activities become possible. Some may extend hobbies like photography, some pass on various skills by training others, some work with charities, some take up writing or become cinema buffs. If envisaged and supported by the city authority, we can imagine a thriving, interactive, inspirational community. Moreover, this will have a positive ecological effect. Currently we rely on more jobs to provide income to people. Unless we can guarantee that all new jobs will be totally green, then pushing up employment – and therefore production and consumption – will increase the exploitation of nature's resources and create further polluting emissions.

Current experience from pilots of basic income in city life are illuminating. Ireland has introduced a basic income for artists, to support the arts sector in its recovery from the Covid-19 pandemic. The Irish government has allocated €25 million to provide €325/month to 2,000 artists chosen by random selection for three years. The impact for artists involved in the scheme will be monitored against a control group. A similar scheme in San Francisco has allocated $1,000/month to 100 artists, whilst the Andrew W Mellon Foundation has launched a $125 million project to give $1,000/month to 2,400 artists across New York state. Meanwhile a basic income pilot has been introduced in Wales for 18-year-olds leaving care. The scheme pays £1,600/month for 24 months to around 500 recipients, costing £20 million in total, and is being evaluated by the Children's Social Care Research and Development Centre at Cardiff University.

The most widespread basic income pilot projects focussing on a city population are in the USA. Stanford UBI Lab reports that about 100 US cities now have a UBI pilot. One of the earliest in Stockton, California, starting in 2019, reported improved mental health and financial stability for recipients at its halfway point. In the UK, two micro-pilots paying £1,600/month to 15 people are proposed in Jarrow and East Finchley. However, in June 2023, the project reported that no funding had been found for the £1.65 million scheme cost. Recipients would be taxed on the payment, and would keep their current welfare benefits, meaning that no comparison of conditionality vs universality would be gained. It's possible that a cross-sectional study across different income groups might generate research findings more immediately.

Overall, these pilots are useful in raising public awareness of the basic income proposal. Their careful research methodologies mean that significant outcomes will be rigorously tested and reported. Initial results already show an increase in wellbeing for recipients, without any substantial decrease in labour market participation. Since each pilot differs in its target recipient group, and in its provision and conditionality, a wide set of findings for basic income against multiple criteria will be generated for comparison, research, and feedback for future scheme proposals.

The limitations of pilot UBI projects are that they are necessarily neither universal, nor unconditional, nor permanent, thus failing to test essential elements of the UBI concept. They may give some indicative data on the economics of basic income but are unable to test the full macroeconomic impact. Pilot schemes lack a proposed pathway from the pilot to full implementation in the national macroeconomy, thus running the risk of terminating without a forward strategy and kicking the UBI concept into the long grass.

We're entitled to dream. Perhaps we can dream together of a future city whose citizens have secure adequate income, who are released from the ravages of low pay, of in-work poverty, of harsh conditional welfare, whose dignity is restored by greater equality in their city society, who flourish in creative individual, communal and civic activity, all whilst reducing ecological damage in a net zero world? Perhaps we can even have such a dream come true? A universal, unconditional, basic income is an important enabling element of this dream. ◼

Geoff Crocker writes on basic income at www.ubi.org and contributes to research on the macroeconomic feasibility of universal basic income and debt-free sovereign money. His career started at Rolls-Royce Bristol, and then spanned several decades in technology strategy, consulting for government agencies, large multinationals and small and medium-sized enterprises. He worked on transition of the Russian economy for 16 years. He is also Chair of Bristol Care Homes.

Q Watch *Free Money*, a documentary which shows the impact of a UBI scheme on the Kenyan village of Kogutu https://homecinema.curzon.com/film/free-money/

"Basic income addresses the social injustice of inequality of today's city."

3.3

How Bristol Could Become the World's Most Inclusive City

Dominic Ellison

Bristol has a prominent place in the history of Disabled people's activism. I'm honoured to work for WECIL (West of England Centre for Inclusive Living), one of the Disabled People's Organisations (DPOs) emerging from the Avon Coalition of Disabled People, whose campaigning for 'Rights Not Charity' in the 1980s and 1990s transformed the city's service provision and contributed significantly to national work securing new rights for Disabled people in the Disability Discrimination Act (later the Equalities Act) and the Care Act, which gave Disabled people implicit rights to choose to remain part of mainstream society and avoid institutionalisation.

While we continue to fight to safeguard our rights to equal inclusion on local and national stages, I observe the Disabled People's Movement failing to harness the key allyship that underpins the light being shone by other equalities movements that are bringing attention to important issues and creating a more just and equitable society. My vision for Bristol is a city grasping the mantle in this key moment of social progression to support Disabled people's advancement from reliance on a safety net of rights-in-law to the comfortable expectation of inclusion on an equal basis to non-disabled people in their day-to-day lives.

Key to this is what we understand 'disability' to mean. One way of thinking about disability is that a person is born 'faulty' (or becomes faulty due to accident, illness or age). In this thinking, someone is diagnosed and becomes labelled as a 'Person with a Disability'. Their 'faultiness' becomes the focus, and their ordinary needs are put on hold as they are segregated and provided alternative services – with a hope of re-entering society should these efforts support them to become 'normal' enough. This thinking largely underscores what we mean when we talk about the Medical Model of Disability.

The model through which DPOs and the wider Disabled People's Movement views disability is known as the Social Model of Disability, which recognises that people are Disabled not because they are somehow deficient, but due to the barriers we have created as a society. It is then an anathema to talk of a person 'having a disability', because disability is not inherent to the individual. Disabled people have impairments (which may be physical, sensory, or cognitive), but it is in the lack of effort to be inclusive of everyone's needs that makes a person Disabled. Where the Medical Model focuses on what is 'wrong' with a person, the Social Model focuses on what is wrong with society.

This is beyond semantics. If, as an employer, I recognise that a candidate cannot fully perform the role they have applied for because they 'have a disability', then surely there is little I can do about it – I'm not a doctor after all. However, when viewed through the Social Model, if a Disabled person applies for a role and it transpires that the work would be inaccessible to them, the responsibility is mine to work with the applicant to identify and remove the barriers that exclude them. If, incidentally, you are an employer who finds this does not apply to you as you don't receive applications from Disabled people, it is your responsibility to identify and remove the barriers preventing one in five people from seeking to join your workforce.

A colleague recently provided consultancy for a housing association to advise on upgrading their homes to meet the access needs of a wider range of Disabled people. The pushback received was that these improvements would narrow the number of people for whom the homes are suitable as 'non-disabled people don't want to live in a social care setting'. The shocking news is – neither do Disabled people.

Interesting things happen when we design for accessibility. The Independent Living Movement which gave rise to a particular type of DPO – Centres for Independent Living (such as WECIL) – has its origins in Berkeley, California, where in the 1970s activists went out under cover of darkness cutting ramps into kerbs so that wheelchair users could cross through town without assistance. This simple intervention has since been adopted globally and dropped kerbs are now a default feature in our urban landscape, essential not only for wheelchair users, but for anyone navigating the cityscape while, for example, pushing a buggy. This change has had further positive impacts on design – luggage has been reimagined to take advantage of wheel-friendlier environments. We no longer see dropped kerbs as a feature of 'Disabled-friendly pavements', simply of 'better pavements'.

Many technological interventions are now so ubiquitous that we don't recognise that their original purpose was to support people with specific impairments. They have shed their 'assistive technology' label and become base expectations of convenient interaction with our phones, computers and even lightbulbs.

To meet the needs of all its citizens, Bristol must go beyond thinking about how to make society more 'accessible' – with its inevitable biases that separate 'normal' users from those with 'access needs', to thinking in terms of 'inclusion' as a necessity, rather than an enhancement. WECIL promotes the principle of Inclusive Design – a process in which products, services and environments are designed to be usable by as many people as possible.

Bristol has its share of leaders in this space. We The Curious recognised years ago that its visitors did not sufficiently represent the local demographic. It wanted to ensure that it was a safe and welcoming space for everybody and was conscious of the need for change both within the physical environment and its whole identity as an organisation. It started by commissioning support from WECIL's Disability.Inc. consultancy service, including an access audit to ensure the building's major renovation considered its physical accessibility. It added key features such as a Changing Place bathroom, featured on the national Changing Places map. Its large space and hoist opened the museum to Disabled people reliant on such facilities, and by offering its use to everyone, not just its visitors, opened the city centre to many who would find visiting otherwise impossible.

We The Curious recognised that physical accessibility of the building was only the start of its journey to inclusion. 'Inclusive Curious City' is the name of our resulting strategic partnership; its ambition: to work with 'audiences from all backgrounds to harness curiosity as the platform for user-led co-production and influence others to join us in working towards making Bristol the world's most inclusive city'. We The Curious' work with WECIL members to shortlist questions from the people of Bristol inspired installations in the 'Project What If' exhibition in 2021, and it provided a home for a WECIL Peer Support Group's 'Curiosity Club'.

Going beyond notions of 'compliance' and tick-boxes, by working closely with a DPO, We The Curious internalised Disability Equality into its practice, embedded structures to scrutinise inclusion across all services, and developed an organisational voice that underpins a culture of full inclusion.

Around the corner, another leader in the journey to inclusion, Watershed, formed a consortium of Bristol venues that recognised their struggle to achieve accessibility could only be overcome by working directly with people with a lived experience of the challenges they were aiming to tackle. Watershed holds inclusion as a core value across their work and sought support from WECIL in access audits for a major capital redevelopment, policy reviews, assessing its support to Disabled artists and valuing Disabled staff and visitors alike. Our partnership was highlighted in its successful application to the latest round of Arts Council National Portfolio Organisations, as is true for St Pauls Carnival.

Bristol's institutional drive towards Disability Equality reflects how the vanguard of positive societal change is often found in the arts. These organisations are to be celebrated but can only achieve so much in isolation. What is the point of cultural institutions achieving the highest standards of access and inclusion if many Disabled people are unable to visit due to poor public transport links and a streetscape that is dangerous to negotiate by wheelchair, or by people with a visual impairment?

Many key decisions are taken without the involvement of Disabled people. In achieving international recognition for its leadership in cities tackling the climate crisis, Bristol's actions overlooked the needs of people whose genuine reliance on cars to access basic services has made the city centre a wholly inaccessible destination, despite Bristol Disability Equality Forum's expansive work on this.

Bristol's development into a place where Disabled people thrive requires a wide range of Disabled people, representing the full spectrum of impairments, to be included in decision-making about the future of our built environment, transport, housing, health, education, employment, shopping, night-time economy, civic participation and thriving cultural scene.

We can't assume to know what others need. Just as Black Lives Matter demonstrates a need to align behind the leadership of Black people, and MeToo spotlights gender inequities and power dynamics by promoting women's voices, so too Disabled people and their organisations need to be an integral part of decision making to realise Inclusive Curious City's objective of making Bristol the world's most inclusive city – something we can be proud to achieve. ■

Dominic Ellison is Chief Executive of WECIL, one of the UK's largest Disabled People's Organisations supporting Disabled people across the West of England. He is internationally recognised for his previous work in pioneering models of community-leadership in regeneration, economic development and cultural programming as Chief Executive of Hackney Co-operative Developments.

Q Find out more about the work of WECIL https://wecil.org.uk/

"Interesting things happen when we design for accessibility."

3.4

How Can We Make Bristol's Transition a Just One?

Emma Geen

This piece is written in Plain English to make it accessible to more people. Words that might not be clear are in bold to show that an explanation of them can be found in the jargon buster at the end. A longer jargon buster can be found on the Bristol Ideas website.

***

In 2020, there were plans to **pedestrianise** St Marks Road to lower car use and make the air cleaner. Named 2019's 'greatest street in Britain', the road has a strong and diverse community with many successful businesses. Yet those on the road weren't talked to early or fully enough when making the plan, so people grew afraid the changes would mean shops would shut. Though research shows that pedestrianisation tends to be good for businesses, over 4,000 people signed a petition against the plan and when it was dropped many called it a victory 'for the community'.

The case is complicated and a full overview can't be given here. However, it's an important place to start when talking about Bristol's **just transition** because it shows how **environmental** action often fails if it isn't made alongside communities and with justice at its centre.

Just transition is an idea that today is used by everyone from governments to the businesses driving **climate change**, like the **fossil fuel** company Shell. Yet the idea came from American chemical unions in the 1970s and working-class Black and ethnic minority communities affected by the pollution the companies were making, and who had been pushing for environmental action as part of the Black rights movement for many years. These groups understood that many jobs hurt workers, communities and the environment, but they didn't agree with the idea that you could either have environmental action or jobs. Instead, they argued that support could be given so that the changes could happen in a way that meant workers could be moved to other jobs that would be healthier for both them and the planet.

The political and economic situation in which they were working is very different from Bristol's. In some areas where the unions worked, a third of local people worked for fossil fuel and chemical companies. Bristol has some large employers that harm the environment, such as the docks, the Ministry of Defence, Bristol Airport and many aerospace companies, but they don't employ most people in the city. However, recent work, such as that of the Climate Justice Alliance, has been returning to the roots of just transition to show that it's relevant even when there is less risk of jobs being lost, showing that it should be about protecting the rights of both workers and disadvantaged communities. This is important to Bristol, which has made leading **declarations** promising to stop the loss of nature and stop the city adding to climate change by 2030. Meeting these goals will mean big changes that will have an impact on life in every part of the city. Such change can be a threat to communities, but it can also be an opportunity.

It was this thinking that led the Bristol Green Capital Partnership to make the Community Climate Action project, which supports disadvantaged groups to take environmental action in a way that creates benefits for their communities. I led on this for the Bristol Disability Equality Forum and, through many community conversations, co-wrote the world's first community climate action plan by and for Disabled people.

Disabled people are one of the groups most at risk from climate change, yet we are also hurt by environmental action that doesn't think about our needs. For example, Bristol's climate strategy says that car journeys in the city should be lowered by 40 per cent by 2030. This action is important, but if accommodations aren't made it could be bad for Disabled people who will never be able to walk, cycle or use buses. It could also be bad for the many Disabled people who could travel in these ways but can't because Bristol's buses, bike lanes and pavements are often inaccessible. What our plan showed, however, is that environmental action could be good for Disabled people if our needs are thought about. Since Bristol is going to have to make changes to its transport to meet its environmental promises, the city could make it more accessible at the same time for not much more money. This would be a big win for Disabled people, which would be much harder to get if pushed for separately from environmental work.

Transition, if done in a just way, should make our city fairer and healthier. While just transition has become a bit of a business buzzword, the idea belongs to workers, and to **grassroots** and disadvantaged communities. These groups must use it to challenge power and show that we could have a better future. Our current society is unfair and isn't working for many people, so environmental action doesn't mean things will get worse if we push for **utopian** climate action. By utopian I don't mean perfect, fictional or unlikely, but action that understands that we deserve a society that is better for everyone.

This isn't dreaming but being practical. The case of St Marks Road shows that transition won't work if it isn't just. Climate change and the loss of nature are the result of a society that ignores the value of different people, species, ways of living and knowledge to allow them to be misused so that a few businesses can make a lot of money. So fixing climate change isn't possible if we don't start valuing all life. This is particularly important for Bristol, which was built using money from the trade in enslaved people and needs to face the injustice in its past and present if it wants to make a just environmental future.

This thinking has led to the writing of a just transition declaration for Bristol. In 2022, I joined a climate justice exchange to the USA with three other Bristol women working on climate and community – Kirsty Hammond, for the Heart of BS13; Rachel Moffat, for Bristol Energy Network; and Olivia Sweeney, for Black and Green Ambassadors. The trip showed us that our city could lead on just climate change action if it wanted to. On our return we asked the mayor for a just transition declaration to be written for Bristol. It was our belief that this is needed to support the city's Climate Emergency and **Ecological** Emergency declarations and strategies to show what it means for their work to be just.

The mayor supported the idea and told us to write it. What followed was many conversations with disadvantaged communities across the city. These quickly showed how complicated making a fully just transition is for Bristol. While some organisations have a lot more power to make the work happen than others (like local politicians) most groups, from businesses to schools to communities, also have an important role. It would be impossible for us to tell each of these what just action means for them. Yet ways of working did become clear, so we wrote the declaration as ten **principles** that every organisation can sign up to and follow to make their environmental work just. These are:

1. We will include the ideas and knowledge of disadvantaged people in all of our work.
2. We will make sure that everyone can have good future-proof jobs.
3. We will support disadvantaged groups to take action that is good for the planet and nature.
4. We will support individual people to make changes through making the big changes that make it easy for them to act.
5. We will make sure that the costs and benefits of the changes are shared out fairly.
6. We will make our ways of talking accessible.
7. We will act in ways that support the people experiencing the worst climate change and nature loss in other places.
8. We will make sure that everyone is more able to cope with the difficulties made by climate change and nature loss.
9. We will make our physical places good for everyone.
10. We will make our organisation fair and bring the principles from the declaration into our work from the start.

These principles are only the start. To bring the just transition to life and make changes stick, organisations across the city will need to shape their work around the principles and challenge themselves to do better every year. It will mean having tricky conversations without easy answers and pushing back on the laziness that lets old injustices continue. We will need to use our imagination to see how work can be done in new and fairer ways, even when there isn't much money or time.

While cases like St Marks Road hopefully won't happen again, other mistakes will. The transition won't be perfect. What matters is that the city listens and uses failures as a chance to grow. Just transition means accepting that we all need to do better and must learn from people who are different from us. None of this will be easy, but it is exciting and hopeful, because a just transition is about working together to make a fair and healthy Bristol that everyone deserves to live in. ■

JARGON BUSTER

Climate change: The planet is getting dangerously hot because of how people are using dirty fuels like petrol. This is leading to lots of problems locally and around the world.

Declaration: Something that is said to show how someone thinks and feels about something. It is a promise to act in a certain way.

Ecological: To do with nature.

Environmental: Anything that is for the planet and nature.

Fossil fuel: The dirty fuels that are dug up, like oil and gas, that are mostly causing climate change.

Grassroots: Groups and actions that come from everyday people who might not have much power on their own.

Just transition: When a place changes how it works and lives so that it isn't causing damage to the planet and nature, but also makes sure that this is done in a fair way for workers and communities.

Pedestrianise / pedestrianisation: When cars are stopped from using an area and it is changed so it is just for people who are walking or rolling.

Principles: A set of statements that says how something is going to be done. They show what is thought to be important in how something is done.

Utopian: A way of thinking and doing things that aims for a society that works well and where everyone is happy.

Emma Geen is a Disabled climate activist and author. She co-wrote the world's first community climate action plan by and for Disabled people for Bristol.

Q Listen to the Just Transitions podcast from the World Resources Institute
https://www.wri.org/just-transitions/podcast-miniseries-just-transition-action

3.5

Future Cities and Intergenerational Solidarity

Helen Manchester

I have worked with and alongside younger and older people, including having taught in secondary schools and higher education institutions and run research and co-design projects with and alongside older adults in care homes and urban settings. Both groups experience ageism and are often excluded from city decision making and future visioning.

However, when ageism is considered in cities, generations are usually discussed separately. For instance, policy makers and commentators have turned to thinking about 'age friendliness' as vital to the future of our cities as our urban populations are not only growing but also getting older. At the same time there are worries about the voices of children and young people in designing and occupying our city spaces and calls for the need for 'child friendly' cities.

It has been argued that in our current cities we often live, learn, work and play in age-segregated spaces such as schools with increasingly high fences, hospitals tailor-made for children or older adults, playgrounds just for children and gated care home facilities. However, there is nothing inevitable about a future of older adults shut away in care homes and children garrisoned in schools.

Back in 2014, I worked with colleagues to co-produce a manifesto for an 'all-age friendly' city. We wanted to question the idea that the intergenerational contract is broken and argue that all age groups should live alongside each other, occupy the same public spaces and have interests and needs in common.

Others have argued that we have seen an increase in intergenerational tension in our cities. This is fanned by organisations who point out the need to redress issues around the 'fairness between generations'. They argue that while increasing longevity is welcome, government policy must be fair to all generations – old, young or those to come. Often there is a sense here that older people are doing better than younger generations who will have fewer opportunities to buy their own home, fewer retirement rights, be unable to walk into jobs for life, and who will bear the brunt of the climate crisis, a crisis made by older, richer generations in the Global North. And added to this mix are the growing and ongoing systemic inequalities experienced across our city populations, including those related to race and migration, gender, sexualities and disabilities.

The future is a building site

It seems we are up against it in building fair and sustainable intergenerational future cities. However, although powerful actors might want us to believe futures are already set, they are not. Futures have always been debated, planned and materialised. 'Anticipation studies' is a relatively new field in academia, at the centre of which is the idea of an active and reflective relationship with futures that are unknowable. 'The future' is seen as a building site that might involve design or political and social struggle. Futures are also understood as unpredictable, opening up possibilities for unforeseen change and disruption, for alternative futures.

Where, then, might we find the resources for our imagination in building fair and sustainable intergenerational city futures? We could look to the Seventh Generation Principle, common across many North American indigenous peoples, that any time someone makes a decision they should think mindfully and with care and responsibility about its impact on people and the planet seven generations into the future. In Wales, they have created a Future Generations Commissioner, whose job it is to be a guardian for future generations and to encourage policy makers to consider the long-term impact of their decisions. The current commissioner discusses the role of artificial intelligence and technologies in society and what it might mean across generations as well as how to live healthy active lives for longer. The United Nations International Youth Day theme for 2022 was a call to action towards Intergenerational Solidarity: Creating a World for All Ages. In Ghana, older and younger people came together to discuss and challenge ageism, for instance, enabling the learning of traditional knowledges from older adults and the sharing of experiences of ageism. These initiatives might help us all to think across all generations, including those yet to come, in building intergenerational future cities with everyone in mind.

Co-designing intergenerational cities

One of the problems we face is pluralising ideas of the future when dominant voices (government departments and international conglomerates, for instance) have taken over spaces of city futures thinking. It is not easy to think about futures right now in our complex and uncertain world, and I'd argue that there is a need to democratise our opportunities, capacities and capabilities for re-imagining futures.

In building intergenerational city futures it is essential not to be driven by expert forecasts alone, but also to co-design with diverse, cross-generational groups with different lived experiences of the city, now and through history. We need to bring these groups into co-design spaces alongside researchers, policy makers, community sector leaders, designers/artists and developers. We need to make problems and concerns visible, tangible and imaginable in a time where there are high levels of uncertainty and complexity. We must engage in mutual and collective learning and question assumptions in order to work towards desired and preferable futures. Through this process we might surface and ask questions such as: how do different generations and groups understand futures? Who owns the future? How can we live alongside other generations, including those yet to come, who understand and practise things differently? Who else needs to be involved in our design conversations? How might we act locally whilst not forgetting our global ties, histories and connections? This is difficult, emotional and maybe slow work that must involve care, trust building and long-term commitments.

I hope that the all-age friendly manifesto we created back in 2014 might be a useful resource in encouraging this intergenerational future city making work to spring up. We co-created seven manifesto principles:

1. A commitment to challenging assumptions about people based on age.
2. Representation and voice of children, young people and senior citizens in democratic processes and citizenship while recognising the diversity of these groups.
3. The experience and perception of safety in the city, including physical, economic and psychological safety, for children, young people and senior citizens.
4. A sense of ownership of the city, in particular its public spaces and buildings, and feelings of belonging, being considered and being welcome in these spaces.
5. A liveable city that encourages independent mobility and positive, pleasurable participation in public and cultural life.
6. Planning processes and advocates who encourage beneficial opportunities for interactions between children, young people and older adults in all areas of education, health, family and civic life.
7. Recognition that poverty and inequality have significant negative impacts upon people of all ages.

These principles are only a starting point for conversations and actions. We must recognise the ambivalences around intergenerational connection in the present. We need to engage with and understand material differences in older and younger people's being in the world in the present that are informed by experiences of the past and of futures. And we have to consider how generational experiences intersect with other social differences including class, race, ethnicity, gender, disabilities and sexualities. We might start with the cities in which we live but we also need to consider questions of transnational intergenerational solidarity and justice. I hope you are up to the challenge. ■

Helen Manchester is Professor of Participatory Sociodigital Futures at the University of Bristol. She is interested in participatory futures, ageing and intergenerational practice, co-design, social connectivity, culture and the arts. She develops methodologically innovative approaches to research in collaboration with artists, technologists, civil society organisations and policy-makers.

Q Find out about the work of the Centre for Ageing Better. What changes you could make in your home and community? https://ageing-better.org.uk/

"...there is nothing inevitable about a future of older adults shut away in care homes and children garrisoned in schools."

3.6

What Does It Mean to Care?

Sian Norris

What does it mean to care?

Right across the UK, everyone from decision-makers and lawmakers to venture capitalists, children and parents is asking this deceptively simple question. With an ageing population, more people living longer with life-limiting conditions and more families and councillors struggling to make budgets add up, the question of care is one of those that will define Bristol's future.

Today, in 2023, there are 61,000 older people living in Bristol, and 8,400 people aged over 85 – although not all are in need of care. More than 750 children are in the care system, and at the end of 2021/2022, there were 2,253 working-age adults in receipt of some form of social care. If Bristol follows national trends, those numbers are set to go up and up.

Their life experiences, their chances of a happy and healthy future, depend on city leaders, citizens and families answering the question: what does it mean to care?

But while the numbers of those in need of care are rising, the amount of money councils have to spend on care has fallen. This has resulted in what some experts call 'the graph of doom', where the net expenditure on care is becoming further and further removed from funding available. Exacerbated by more than a decade of austerity – where grants from central to local government were almost halved on average – the gap between spend and need has continued to widen.

'There is a perfect storm when it comes to social care,' explains Councillor Helen Holland. As the cabinet member with responsibility for Adult Social Care and the Integrated Care System, Holland has an excellent insight into the needs, pressures and solutions for care in the city. 'There are more people in need of care, sometimes very expensive care. There are cost pressures, rising costs across the board means care providers are asking for more. And there are workforce shortages.'

Care providers are seeing a widening gap between the money offered per person from the council and the day-to-day running costs of running a residential care home or care service. Sometimes that gap can be as much as £200 per person.

Another storm brewing is linked to the crisis in the health service.

More and more people are living with conditions for longer before getting treated, requiring more complex care for longer. Then there's the 'bed blocking' issue, where people have no choice but to stay in hospital for longer after an incident – be that an injury or illness – due to a lack of social care places to move patients into. The longer someone remains in hospital, the more complex the recovery. Some trusts are resorting to extreme measures, moving patients into temporary hotel placements to relieve the pressure on wards and ease the 'bed blocking'.

The result of this perfect storm of pressure, Holland warns, is that local authorities can end up doing things wrong, because they don't have the resources to innovate and improve.

The doom graph may be the focus of local and central governments, but Holland is keen to emphasise that the outlook on social care does not have to be gloomy. She is keen to promote innovation and inclusion across the sector, to ensure more people with complex needs can get the most out of life.

One example of innovation in adult social care in the West of England is the We Work For Everyone campaign, which supports learning disabled people into the workforce. The initiative also supports employers to make the necessary adaptations to support their new staff member.

A combination of practical barriers as well as longstanding discrimination means that Disabled adults, and learning disabled adults in particular, are locked out of employment. They may be eager to work and have the skills to work, but stigma means doors are closed in their faces. The We Work For Everyone campaign breaks down those barriers.

It may sound unrelated, but supporting people who want to work into work is a form of care. It recognises that every person has different needs, skills and aspirations for their life, within the care system and outside of it. While not everyone living with complex needs can work, or indeed wants to, some do, and their ambitions deserve support and respect.

'The response has been fantastic,' explains Holland. 'With people being able to live independently, feeling that they're contributing to society.'

Work is one thing. But building a city that has care at its heart requires a broader approach that recognises our shared civic responsibility to the most vulnerable in society.

This means investing in open and accessible city infrastructure that supports a wide range of people's needs, from the parent negotiating a buggy on the bus to get their child to the local library, to local parks where older people can enjoy a sit-down in the fresh air, and community centres offering classes and social sessions. Care does not need to happen in a residential home or a hospital bed. It can happen in every corner of our city.

The idea that care can be central to a city and its infrastructure is something that drives Geoff Crocker. It's now more than 20 years since Crocker set up Bristol Care Homes, which are dedicated to providing affordable social care for older people.

'We need to be engaging the care home community – and that means residents, relatives, and staff – into civic society,' says Crocker. Rather than seeing care as something that happens to specific people in discrete areas, there is a need to bring care into society, making it something we are all engaged in.

In common with the whole sector, Bristol Care Homes is facing many challenges. The ongoing impact of the Covid-19 pandemic along with the cost-of-living crisis and workforce shortages have all put pressure on the business. And providing care is, in itself, a challenging space to operate in.

'There are a number of people in the community who are elderly and have lost capacity to some degree,' says Crocker. 'This could be mobility, it could be to do with incontinence, it could be to do with loss of intellectual capacity and dementia. Caring for people in those situations is fairly challenging, because unlike a hospital, a care home is providing long-term care, usually for the rest of a person's life. That is both holistic and clinical care.'

In the face of these pressures, Bristol Care Homes has committed to innovation, so it can meet both its residents' needs and the needs of their wider families, all while helping to build a Bristol that puts care at its heart.

Driving that spirit of innovation is the understanding that older people today are not the same older people as of our childhoods. Today's pensioners are not the stereotypes of days gone by – they require different entertainment, engagement and activities than previous generations.

'We don't patronise the elderly person, we don't stereotype the elderly person and we don't project our own preferences onto the elderly person,' explains Crocker. In practice, this means devising an activities programme that meets older people where they are, offering art classes, music sessions (with the playlist ranging from classical harpists to The Rolling Stones) and trips on long boats and to falconry centres, as well as regular visits to the garden centre. One memorable occasion, which Crocker hopes will become an annual event, was an immersive Aurora Orchestra concert in Bristol Cathedral that brought the city and care residents together.

Such on-the-ground innovations help to keep residents active and engaged, help staff enjoy their time at work and offer relatives peace of mind. But there is a need, Crocker and Holland agree, for more structural innovations that meet the graph of doom head on and ensure that an ageing population, and a rising number of adults and children in care, get the support they need to live happy, healthy and fulfilled lives.

Such structural reform can start with tackling a seemingly unrelated issue: socioeconomic inequality. Bristol remains a deeply divided city, with council wards struggling with extreme deprivation set cheek-by-jowl with wards where incomes and house prices soar.

Healthy life expectancy for men and women in Bristol is below the national average, and people living in the most deprived areas have a lower healthy life expectancy than those in wealthier wards. The gap in healthy life expectancy between the most deprived ten per cent and the least deprived ten per cent within Bristol is 16.3 years for males and 16.7 years for females, and there are five areas where male healthy life expectancy is in the lowest five per cent in England. These are Knowle West, Barton Hill, Withywood, Upper Easton and Hartcliffe. For women, there are three areas that fall within the lowest five per cent: Withywood, Hartcliffe and Barton Hill.

The gap in healthy life expectancy is a warning. The longer people live with complex long-term health conditions, the more care they need. To build a caring future for Bristol depends on us building a more equal one. ■

Sian Norris is a writer and investigative journalist who has covered far-right movements and their relocation to the mainstream for a range of publications, including the UK's *Times* newspaper and *The Observer*. She is the author of *Bodies Under Siege: How the Far-Right Attack on Reproductive Rights Went Global*. In 2012 she set up the Bristol Women's Literature Festival, which she ran for eight years.

Q Access support for those caring and being cared for
https://www.bristol.gov.uk/residents/social-care-and-health/carers/support-for-carers

"...building a city that has care at its heart requires a broader approach that recognises our shared civic responsibility to the most vulnerable in society."

3.7

How Do We Create a City That Is Just?

Alex Raikes, written with Anna Wardell

I was young when I first witnessed racism. I grew up in a mixed heritage and mixed skin colour family with a white British mum and Kurdish-Iranian father who had fled to the UK. Whilst I was light-skinned, my father and brother were not. When I was four, we moved from multicultural South East London to a predominantly white, working-class, rural area where we were one of only a few minority ethnic families. Racial abuse was a daily experience, and included physical attacks against my brother, discrimination across the board for my father (which carried on wherever he went when he left the family unit) and relentless verbal abuse towards me. I quickly learned to negotiate and argue my way out of the bullying I faced but it wasn't so easy for my brother or father. There were lots of repercussions including mental health issues, family breakdown and a feeling of being outsiders.

These experiences have informed my life's work, inspiring me with a determination and passion for promoting human rights and doing what I can so that others do not have to go through what I did, or are at least supported and believed when they do. Sadly, joining Stand Against Racism & Inequality (SARI), a leading regional hate crime charity, has made it clear to me that we still have a long way to go. Far too many people continue to suffer at the hands of a minority of people who view the richness that diversity brings to the world as a threat.

SARI was set up by a steering group of local people who wanted to make Bristol a more just city for its minority ethnic communities. These pioneers included victims of racial harassment such as parents, business owners, a local Black reverend, a director of a Black housing association and SARI's wonderful founding director, Batook Pandya. They shared a common understanding that dealing with racism often led to coming up against a brick wall, criminalisation and frequently an inadequate response from agencies, which were at best unable to understand their plight and at worst institutionally racist and complicit in the abuse. Victims were alone and vulnerable.

Support Against Racist Incidents, as it was known then, secured its first funding in 1991. I joined as SARI's first caseworker that year, aged 22 and fresh out of university.

Already in post was Agnes Yeomans, who sorted all the back office and administrative needs of SARI and who is now our finance and HR director, and Batook, SARI's first director, who sadly passed away in 2014.

Batook was instrumental in SARI becoming the highly regarded charity it is today. He was a tireless campaigner for justice in our city and renowned for his honest, outspoken, multi-agency approach to fighting racism. He believed that you had to work with agencies such as the police and local authorities who had the power to make the difference. However, he was determined that SARI clients had to be firmly in the driving seat. As our chair at the time of his death, Esther Deans, stated, 'Batook believed passionately in creating a better society by working together, not against each other, which is why there is such a need to overcome the crippling injustices that divide us – a community divided by discrimination can never be a community united.' Losing him was a huge blow personally and professionally. It is in his honour that I continue ensuring SARI does all it can to fight hate in all its insidious forms.

In our first year, we opened and supported 44 racial harassment cases. Batook and I were out day and night, visiting those who were being attacked in almost every way you can imagine. Many stick in my mind, including a young Pakistani man, Tariq Hussain, who had a finger and thumb slashed off in a vicious, unprovoked racist attack by a group of white men when he was on his way back from work, and a spate of 80-plus attacks across the Fishponds area when a far-right group ran a racist campaign to target anyone in the telephone directory with a foreign-sounding name. Our cases leave an imprint and constant reminder that we must do better, and that communities and agencies must unite to prevent and reduce hatred which, if left unchecked, can go to very dark places, as we saw with atrocities such as the Holocaust and the Rwandan genocide.

Fast-forward 31 years, and we are a diverse team of 23 staff, all dedicated to tackling hate across Avon and Somerset. We remain led by a board, nearly all of whom have lived experience of hate. Each year, we deal with up to 900 referrals and open around 400 cases, reaching thousands more via our signposting, education, awareness and outreach work.

SARI has adapted to the changing times. Whilst we started out focussed solely on victims of racism, we have expanded our focus to support people dealing with all types of hate crime, changing our name to Stand Against Racism & Inequality to reflect this shift. We also collaborate with specialist partners, recognising that we needed new expertise and new lived experience for LGBTQ+ and Disabled people.

SARI was created in the context of a long-divided city that was built on the suffering of those who were enslaved; much of Bristol's wealth comes from exploitation and trauma. In the decades before our creation, we saw the Bristol Bus Boycott, a successful movement for justice against the deeply unfair colour bar that relied on the actions of ordinary people to overturn. And in the 1990s, as SARI was formed, we witnessed a wave of civil unrest with uprisings happening across the country, including in St Pauls in Bristol due to unfair policing and discrimination of the UK's Black communities.

Bristol's reputation on the national and global stage complements and contrasts with its everyday reality. We have lots to be proud of regarding campaigns for justice but, despite our reputation as a trendy, edgy, diverse and multicultural city, there is also discord and discontent lying beneath the surface. According to the Runnymede report *Drifting Upwards or Sliding Back*, we were the seventh most unequal city in the UK in terms of racial equality in 2011. We have witnessed truly awful acts of injustice and hate in our city, including the violent assault of Black teenager Marlon Thomas in 1993, when a group of white men set out to deliberately target young Black people at a funfair. In the past ten years we have seen two racist murders of people who came to our city seeking safety and sanctuary – Bijan Ebrahimi, murdered on 14 July 2013, and Kamil Ahmad Ali, murdered on 7 July 2016. The very fact that SARI has to exist, and that it is as busy as it is, is a demonstration of how far our city still needs to come.

That isn't to say that there aren't great things happening in Bristol. We are also one of the most innovative, compassionate and wonderful cities when it comes to striving for justice. In my role as Strategic Director at SARI, and during my year as High Sheriff of Bristol 2022-2023, I was privileged to see this. From Creative Youth Network's Welcome Wednesdays, a drop-in for unaccompanied asylum-seeker minors, to volunteers of all ages and backgrounds working together in a dilapidated warehouse to get donations across to Ukraine, to Youth Moves' teenage leaders coordinating funding for local people in need, I have seen some of the best of humanity in Bristol. This dedication and passion galvanises me to keep on fighting for justice.

There is much to keep us hopeful. As I said in my introduction to my pioneering event as High Sheriff, A Lifetime for Justice, 'every meaningful step towards...improved human rights, has been pre-empted by ordinary citizens with fire in their bellies. People who have been unwavering, persistent and relentless in their quest for a fairer society. Often fuelled by their own experiences of brutal injustice, these are the people who have pledged their life to justice.'

So, what do we need to do to create a city that is just? We need determination and persistence. We need everyone to share the responsibility for seeking justice. We need many people achieving small acts that combine to make their community safer and fairer. This can be in any sphere: school, workplace, place of worship, local pub. You can contribute to equality and justice in each of these life locations. You can advocate for better systems for dealing with bullying and hate anywhere. You can organise inclusive celebrations which embrace diversity. You can be a committee member, a governor, a volunteer, a parishioner, or do a walk or run for charity.

It is the god of small steps that make a city more just. As Eleanor Roosevelt said: 'Where, after all, do universal human rights begin? In small places, close to home – so close and so small that they cannot be seen on any maps of the world. Yet they are the world of the individual person; the neighborhood [they live] in; the school or college [they attend]; the factory, farm, or office where [they work]... Unless these rights have meaning there, they have little meaning anywhere. Without concerted citizen action to uphold them close to home, we shall look in vain for progress in the larger world.' This is my life mantra – can you make it yours? ■

Alex Raikes was the first caseworker at Stand Against Racism & Inequality (SARI), a leading regional hate crime charity. She is now their Strategic Director and continues to be a driving force in the city in tackling racism and hate crime. She was awarded an MBE in 2009 for her contribution to race relations, made an Honorary Doctor of Laws by UWE Bristol in 2019, became a Deputy Lieutenant of Bristol in July 2020 and was High Sheriff of Bristol 2022-2023.

Anna Wardell is Communications and Fundraising Officer at Stand Against Racism & Inequality (SARI).

Q Find out more about the work of SARI https://saricharity.org.uk/

"...what do we need to do
to create a city that is just?
We need determination
and persistence.
We need everyone
to share the responsibility
for seeking justice.."

3.8

What Happened to the Ladder? Social Mobility in Bristol

Annabel Smith

Looking only at the crudest of gross domestic product (GDP) measures, you could be forgiven for characterising Bristol's economic growth story as one of unabated success: it is one of the only UK cities that is a net contributor to Treasury. Other than Glasgow, it is the only city outside London in which there are more people with degrees than people without them. Its culture sector is globally celebrated. It is a strikingly young city, with a median age of 32.4 compared to the national average of 40.2, marking it as somewhere that talented, educated young people from across the country and across the world choose to make their home. At the same time, it is a city that is proudly diverse, with at least 45 religions, 187 countries of birth and 91 main languages spoken by people living here. But who gets a stake in contributing to and benefiting from the city's economic success is a hotly contested issue.

It is not uncommon to hear Bristol referred to as 'a tale of two cities'. It has some of the most profound socioeconomic, racial and spatial inequalities in the country. For a city with fewer than half a million residents, the extent to which your life outcomes are dependent on where in Bristol you happen to be born, who your parents are, the colour of your skin and the school you attend is remarkable. In 2017, the government's Social Mobility Commission ranked Bristol as one of the least socially mobile urban areas in the country, placing it in the worst performing ten per cent of local authorities for people from disadvantaged backgrounds going on to improved life outcomes. For a place filled with educated young people from outside its boundaries, a woeful one in 60 of the disadvantaged young people who grow up here will go on to attend a highly selective university such as the one right on their doorstep: the University of Bristol. With education levels seen as one of the key markers of social mobility, the spatial divisions here are prominent, with almost all pupils in Clifton and Redland progressing to higher education as opposed to just 8.7 per cent in Hartcliffe – one of the lowest-performing neighbourhoods in England. On racial inequality, the city performs similarly poorly, with a landmark study by the Runnymede Trust in 2017 (*Bristol: A City Divided?*) ranking Bristol the seventh most racially unequal local authority out of 348 in the country, and the most unequal of all Core Cities (the 11 biggest cities outside London).

This is not to say that Bristol's poor performance in bridging inequalities stands in contrast to an exemplary national picture. The UK's experience of recent years, characterised by political and economic turmoil and economic shocks, has shown that national progress on social mobility is not linear. In fact, mobility has now been stalling for several years, with wealth inequality across generations persistently high across the UK. And, while research shows that the children of higher-earning parents go on to earn more themselves, it is wealth – not just earnings – that marks the clearest dividing line. Even among those whose parents earn the same amount, children of parents with more wealth are more likely to go on to earn more themselves and to reach the top of the wealth distribution. Given this, we need to think about social mobility not just in terms of generation-on-generation earning power, but in terms of assets and ownership. In a rentier economy, this means that even as today's young person makes all of the decisions they have been told by society will lead to upward mobility, the goal posts of economic security are continually shifting out of reach.

This poses a major challenge for the future of social mobility in Bristol, because the main route to achieving wealth – property ownership – is increasingly unattainable through decent wages alone. This is a national problem but is particularly acute here. Having seen some of the highest increases in the UK, property prices in Bristol have effectively doubled over the past decade. This would not be as prohibitive a barrier to mobility if we had an adequate social housing stock, or devolved powers for the local authority to impose the rent controls that would help to curb our overheated and underregulated private rental market, both of which the local authority has lobbied the government hard for.

With this double problem of deep-seated inequality and a worsening housing crisis, we are standing dangerously close to the precipice of an entrenched reality for Bristol, whereby economic security is the preserve of the intergenerationally wealthy. If there is a social mobility ladder, only its first few rungs are assailable now. How many will there be for future generations to climb?

All of this reflects my own experience. Born in the early nineties to a single parent on a council estate in Blackburn, a post-industrial town in North West England with some of the worst child poverty rates in the country, university was not only something of which my family had no experience, but a distant concept I never considered a real possibility. One thing poverty and instability robs you of is the luxury of thinking too far into the future beyond survival. It was only a chance meeting with a persistent college careers adviser adamant that 'you should be going to Oxbridge!' that nudged the course of my life onto a markedly different path. Thanks to the lightbulb ignited by this comment, an encouraging mum and a few years of determined study funded by loans and part-time work, I found myself with a ticket to the gates of upward mobility – an Oxbridge degree.

As a recent graduate sleeping at my mum's mouldy rented studio flat, with the resolution that I would forge a career trying to play a part in addressing the structural inequities I had seen and experienced first-hand, I lacked the social capital and connections to land me a role in Westminster. It was seeing the incumbent mayor of Bristol speaking passionately to these issues on the national news that drew me, like so many other young people, to our city in 2017. A Black man of mixed heritage raised in poverty by a single mother in Bristol, Marvin Rees was the type of politician whose relative absence was conspicuous on the national stage. I was inspired by his vision. Luckily, there happened to be a paid internship advertised in his office at the time. Having secured the position, in no small part due to speaking of my own story of burgeoning social mobility in the interview, a door was cracked open for me in Bristol.

Working alongside a mayor whose fundamental mission is that of tackling the city's socioeconomic, spatial and racial inequities, I was afforded the opportunity to build social capital from scratch in a way that would have been far more challenging in London. With Rees centralising opportunity creation in his leadership approach, I was able to make progress into increasingly senior roles and was entrusted to lead on mayoral priorities close to my heart, such as programmes to tackle adverse childhood experiences and period poverty. The nature of collaborative city governance fostered by Rees – characterised by the One City Approach – meant that lived experience was regarded as an asset in those with a role in making decisions about the city's future. The experience and connections I built during this time at City Hall enabled me to move into a senior role at a Westminster think tank, while continuing to call Bristol home and work with organisations in the city on issues related to economic inclusion. This would not have been possible without a foot in the door from a city administration committed to ensuring nobody is left behind. But, despite Bristol providing a springboard in so many ways, the security of home ownership and escape from the insecure rental market remains elusive, as is the case for thousands of others in the same boat.

For the social contract of social mobility to be strengthened in the future rather than torn up further, local leaders, politically but also across all sectors, need to continue to prioritise tackling inequality, ensuring a joined-up approach to addressing other challenges such as the transition to net zero, and bringing everybody along on that journey. In terms of what national government can do, alongside an industrial strategy that would help make business investment as attractive as property ownership for wealth creation, those with skin in the game who understand the complexities of Bristol's challenges need to be given the tools and the trust to make the long-term decisions that would meaningfully turn the tide. This means being able to take a whole place approach to enhancing business investment while driving the improvements in health, housing, skills and education that underpin social mobility.

And at a time when young people are significantly worse off than older generations were at their age, governments must have more commitment to redressing radical disparity between age groups. A starting point would be to take seriously recent recommendations from the Intergenerational Commission, including meaningfully reforming the rental market to give renters better rights and protections, reform of the capital gains and inheritance tax systems that are currently helping to entrench inequality, and a new regime for property tax that taxes more wealth at a lower threshold. A brave shift that meaningfully makes way for mobility is not a 'nice to have', but vital to securing our city's future success story as one that we can all contribute to and benefit from. ■

Annabel Smith is Head of Place and Practice at the Centre for Progressive Policy, an economic think tank focussed on driving fair growth across the UK.

Q Read about and contribute to the Social Mobility index to understand how social mobility is affecting where you live https://index.socialmobility.org.uk/

"A brave shift that meaningfully makes way for mobility is not a 'nice to have', but vital to securing our city's future success story as one that we can all contribute to and benefit from."

3.9

How Can Bristol Support Nature Recovery?

Savita Willmott

I believe that when the Covid-19 pandemic brought Bristol to a standstill in March 2020, our relationship with nature changed. I know mine certainly did. My strongest memory of those early days of a global pandemic is taking my nine-month-old from our city-centre flat to Queen Square to give him some much-needed practice crawling on grass. It was only a few minutes before we were sent home by a police officer monitoring the square with a reminder that only one hour of outdoor exercise was permitted under current restrictions. The unexpected experience of being suddenly cut off from nature, even in its most basic form in a city-centre Georgian square, would stay with me years later, and directly influence my charity's environmental communication activities and campaigns.

Back to Covid-19: in 2020, the media was filled with stories of wildlife emerging onto empty streets and birdsong finally being heard in the city centre. These stories, full of awe and wonder, would eventually give way to images of overflowing waste bins and stories of trying to socially distance on mountaintops and in forests.

It was in February 2020, only a month before the first Covid-19 restrictions, that Bristol became the first city to declare an 'ecological emergency'. A companion to the climate strategy launched in the city the year before, the declaration set out how intrinsically linked the challenges were. Now that so many cities and regions have followed, it's easy to forget how forward-thinking it was to clearly outline that we could make progress on our climate targets but that if biodiversity collapsed we would still face dire consequences. The declaration itself makes for sobering reading: Bristol's songbirds, such as swifts and starlings, wiped out by 96 per cent between 1994 and 2014. Between 60 per cent of wild invertebrates and up to 76 per cent of insects wiped out around the world since 1970.

I've been working in environmental communications for 20 years, leading The

Natural History Consortium, a charitable collaboration of Bristol-based and national organisations working together on a common mission of engaging people with the natural world. Facts, figures and statistics are important and illustrative tools, but they can also obscure, mislead or confuse our audiences. However, I've always liked the choice of these two evocative facts and have had many conversations with people who recall 'having more insects on the windshield' or 'hearing more birds in the city' in the past or when they were young. Words matter. Even the term 'ecological emergency' can sound out of step with more familiar terminology such as 'nature' or 'wildlife'. Some collaborators were concerned with the use of the word 'emergency' as we already found ourselves in a global pandemic.

These points were front of mind when, over the spring and summer of 2020, a group of representatives from 39 different organisations across the city sat down to write a city-wide strategy for addressing our ecological emergency. It was, by necessity, written remotely and online, through a summer of changing restrictions.

To my surprise, pulling the strategy together turned out to be more straightforward than I expected. There was broad – if not total – agreement that we already knew what needed to be done, and that the primary aim of the strategy was to set it out clearly in a way that demonstrated the role that all individuals and organisations in the city have. Here is what we broadly agreed.

First, people and organisations across Bristol need to combine resources to create bigger, better and more joined-up habitats for nature. Bristol's strategy echoes national and international targets, calling for 30 per cent of the city to be dedicated as 'space for nature' by 2030.

Second, we need to stop degrading and destroying our current habitats. The strategy for Bristol focuses on reducing pesticide use in the city by 50 per cent by 2050, and explores the health of our waterways. The strategy also calls on individuals, organisations and businesses to consider and reduce the 'wider footprint' of their purchasing and procurement decisions that may affect habitats around the globe, and this has sparked fascinating discussions inside and outside the city.

Whatever clarity we may have had about what needed to be done, how to reach these targets – together, as a city – is an ongoing debate and discussion. From my perspective, the strategy is written very much with the 'emergency' perspective in mind. It sets out where the city should aim, and does not make recommendations around, for example, baseline measurements.

The Natural History Consortium mission is 'engaging people with the natural world through collaborative action', and our focus is on environmental communications and engagement. As Bristol celebrates its 650th anniversary, our charity celebrates its 20th. Our annual Festival of Nature continues to celebrate wildlife in the city, but also to encourage and track individual 'actions for nature' – increasingly targeted to the specific calls in this strategy document.

In 2021 we experimented with a 'pesticide amnesty', an event in partnership with

University of Bristol and Bristol Waste that attracted regional and national press coverage. The idea was simple: provide mobile disposal (with a specialist chemical team) in two areas to invite people to empty their houses and allotment sheds of pesticides. We were surprised that what people brought was often very old, dripping bottles of chemicals, many without labels, and sometimes inherited from previous shed owners on an allotment.

I sat on the welcome desk for two days. The crucial learning for me was that the majority of people who visited and openly shared their views about pesticide use were nature lovers. I spoke with many people who were keen to create beautiful gardens and outdoor spaces. Many were unaware of the damage that herbicides (chemicals sprayed on plants) could have on insects, especially when there was a nice friendly bee on the label. Many pet owners were also unaware of the impact of flea sprays on Bristol's insect population. We have published our findings from the event and held a number of conversations with other cities about our work. Our city's local recycling centres have chemical collections throughout the year, but the weekend experiment allowed us to speak to people directly and inform future communications activity.

There are a huge number of projects, organisations and campaigns across the city. Festival of Nature involved over 100 organisations and groups this year, and there are many more. Responses to the city's annual 'Quality of Life' survey demonstrate that people are aware of their impact on the natural world, eager to spend time in it and believe that they are taking action for nature. Avon Wildlife Trust has created Team Wilder, based on recent research around creating societal tipping points for change – in this case, collective individual action for nature. Momentum is growing and progress is being made.

Yet there are great challenges too. Future Bristolians looking back at 2023 will find that the main discussions about our 'ecological emergency' today are around difficult questions regarding land use, housing and local green spaces. These debates are hugely important, and better recorded by others more closely involved. Access to nature and diversity in decision making require difficult discussions and faster progress. Our wildlife and green spaces are critically important to the one in eight people who do not have access to nature.

Bristol 650 gives us an opportunity to look closely at our city, our decision making and our collective work on our biggest challenge. I hope that 2023 will mark a turning point as together we tackle our ecological emergency and support nature's recovery.

In May 2023, we had word from a local volunteer, Susan Acton-Campbell, who shared that she had photographed a bee during our annual 'City Nature Challenge'. During this annual event our charity asked people across Bristol to take photographs and upload them to the iNaturalist website. It's a citizen science effort to help add to our database of wildlife across the city. Susan shared that it seemed she had recorded a bee called *Nomada zonata* in Troopers' Hill, the first time the bee had been found in Bristol. It was hairless, looked rather like a wasp, and was known as a 'cuckoo bee' as it was a type of 'parasite' known as a cleptoparasite. A sighting, only the 113th in the UK and the first in the region, therefore showed that the 'host' species, *Andrena dorsata*, was also present in the city.

Susan's bee sighting highlights the technological revolution of wildlife sighting – a bee was photographed on a mobile phone, uploaded to iNaturalist for one expert opinion and sent over Twitter for another. We need more environmental data, not just collected on iNaturalist but long-term data sets. It's difficult to know how long this type of bee has been living in Bristol – it has only been recorded in the UK since 2017, and the closest previous sighting was in Stroud in 2020. Still, it's a fitting addition to Bristol 650. Welcome to Bristol, *Nomada zonata*. Long may you thrive in our city. ■

Savita Willmott is Chief Executive of the Natural History Consortium. She joined in 2006, managed the transition to charitable status in 2008, and as Chief Executive continues to grow the impact and reach of the projects locally, nationally and internationally.

Q Get involved with the City Nature Challenge and document the natural world around you https://www.citynaturechallenge.org/

"I hope that 2023 will mark a turning point as together we tackle our ecological emergency and support nature's recovery."

4

FUTURE WORK AND FUTURE BRISTOL

Boom City Bristol – But Can It Last?

Martin Boddy

Aerospace giants Airbus and Rolls-Royce; Aardman Animations of Wallace and Gromit fame; the BBC Natural History Unit, home of many of David Attenborough's wildlife blockbusters; and a cluster of finance professional services companies, including KPMG and stockbrokers Hargreaves Lansdown, point to the strength of the Bristol economy across multiple business sectors. Not forgetting leading tech businesses such as Oracle, Cray, fitness app specialist Strava and many more built on the back of early investment by Hewlett Packard and semiconductor pioneer Inmos.

Digging beneath the headlines, Bristol's economy is strong across a whole range of measures. Unemployment is low, both the 'official' claimant count rate and also 'hidden' unemployment, including the long-term sick. The Centre for Cities' Cities Data Tool (which defines the Bristol Urban Area as including the local authority areas of the City of Bristol and South Gloucestershire) shows that Bristol ranks 11th out of 63 towns and cities on productivity, the value of goods and services produced per hour worked. It ranks ninth nationally on its share of 'new economy' jobs in fintech and advanced manufacturing, ninth also for IT and high-value 'knowledge-based' employment. The picture overall has also been one of growth: Bristol's population was up by over ten per cent in the decade to 2021. Numbers of jobs grew by ten per cent over the last five years, making Bristol the fourth fastest-growing urban area nationally. This is particularly significant given that Bristol is a big city – 760,000 people and 460,000 jobs, the fifth largest urban area outside of London on total jobs. The best-performing and fastest-growing places are typically smaller towns and cities, particularly former new towns closer to London, not the big conurbations like Bristol.

Bristol was ranked fourth nationally in PwC's latest *Good Growth for Cities Index*, combining economic indicators like income, jobs and skills along with measures of health, environment, safety and work-life balance. It took first place in the *Sunday Times' 2017 Best Places to Live* (and was termed 'cool, classy and supremely creative') and was voted *Rough Guide*'s Top City in the same year. It was also European Green Capital in 2015.

Why then has Bristol done so well? Historically, Bristol has been able to continuously reinvent itself. It suffered much less than other large urban areas from post-war decline in manufacturing and traditional industries, with less long-lasting scarring of the economy and skills as well as the urban landscape. Relocation from London of office-based professional services and early tech investment, including Hewlett Packard and Inmos, laid the foundations for a dynamic, 'post-industrial' economy. And aerospace, smaller overall in job terms, remains a major cluster of high-value advanced manufacturing.

Stand-out business sectors locally now include professional and legal services, aerospace and advanced manufacturing, creative and media and digital technologies. By no means unique to Bristol, they are, however, relatively large, dynamic and more concentrated locally, certainly in combination, than in much of the rest of the country. Collectively they help give Bristol the edge. Importantly as well, they represent well-developed 'clusters' of the sort seen by economist Michael Porter and a host of analysts and policymakers since as critical to productivity and economic dynamism. Clusters of often interconnected businesses draw on large pools of skills and labour, common supply chains, specialist supports and services and supportive governance structures. Developed over time, these attributes come to constitute a 'deep ecology' of knowledge, innovation, networks, relationships and opportunities which mutually reinforce the benefits to individual businesses.

Many studies have tried to unravel the key factors driving productivity and growth, pointing to a combination of workforce skills; local industry mix; the quality of place, infrastructure and environment; connectivity and location; and local governance and management. Proximity to London, motorway connectivity, high-speed rail (recently electrified) and strong business and cultural links have favoured Bristol both historically and more recently in terms of relocation, investment and expansion, talent acquisition and recruitment and – less tangibly – cultural fit, reputation and visibility. The attractiveness, liveability and lifestyle offered by the city and surrounding countryside has also been key in attracting and retaining people, business and investment. This has included the variety of urban environments and potential lifestyles on offer across the city and beyond, the style of inner suburbs or harbourside living, the 'edginess' of the inner city, proximity to outdoors activities, more conventional suburban areas and beyond to desirable and commutable rural towns and villages.

Ranked 11th nationally for the proportion of the workforce with high-level qualifications, Bristol also has a large pool of labour with the sort of skills and attributes that businesses need to draw on to drive growth and competitiveness. The attractiveness of Bristol in terms of lifestyle and location, combined with the salaries and opportunities on offer in a large, competitive labour market, help businesses recruit and retain staff from elsewhere – both early career and more experienced staff looking to relocate, including from London and internationally. This tends to be self-reinforcing, with high-skill individuals attracted to places which have already demonstrated their attractiveness. The city's two universities, with over 50,000 students between them, are important contributors, providing a regular stream of graduates across a wide range of subjects, boosted by those coming to study from outside of Bristol who take up employment locally. The universities also contribute as major employers in their own right, through support for business innovation and growth and through the value of student spend locally.

Transformation of the fabric of the place has also played a key role. The historic city docks and warehouses transitioned into residential apartments, bars, restaurants and heritage, arts and cultural attractions. The centre of gravity of earlier office-based activity in the city centre has shifted eastwards, with a major cluster of new developments on underused sites towards the main Temple Meads rail station and beyond. Strong market demand has seen reinvestment in and the refurbishment of 'left-behind' buildings in the older urban core as apartments and student accommodation. Bristol's 'northern arc', with outstanding motorway and rail connectivity and historically a more permissive planning regime, also saw strong growth in housing and employment, many thousands employed by the Ministry of Defence, Bristol Science Park, the University of the West of England and major employers at Severnside, including, most recently, Amazon.

Taking the city as a whole, Bristol has clear strengths from an economic perspective. But looking across different parts of the city it is clear that not all have benefited from economic success. Fifteen per cent of the total population of Bristol (over 70,000 people) live in the most deprived ten per cent of areas of England as a whole. There are stark differences in terms of hidden unemployment in particular, while life expectancy in parts of South Bristol is over ten years lower than affluent Clifton and Cotham just north of the city centre. Longstanding social exclusion means that many in the most deprived inner-city areas and outer estates are simply disconnected from the opportunities created by the overall success of the city.

Among other challenges, Bristol's jobs growth and relatively high earnings of those in employment, coupled with limited supply of new housing, has also led to eye-wateringly high house prices and private sector rents. Average house prices have risen to nearly 12 times average incomes, making Bristol eighth worst nationally for affordability. Rents are also amongst the highest outside of London, affecting those for whom ownership is not an option, including those on lower incomes but also mobile early career graduates who might be priced out of the local labour market. The cost of housing is a potential threat to the continued ability of the city to attract and retain both more highly skilled labour and those working in lower-paid service roles. Commentators have suggested that outdated greenbelt provision and planning restraint have potentially had an impact on the growth rate of UK cities and, in the case of Bristol, constrained the supply of both housing and employment land. Difficult politically given 'nimbyist' opposition to new housing, this is, however, a clear threat to continued growth. Nor is it clear that the city could respond to the sorts of major, high-profile inward investment opportunities that have done so much to boost its past success.

Connectivity nationally remains strong with improved journey times to London by rail following recent electrification. But Bristol has never had the major investment in public urban transport seen across all other major cities in the UK and, despite recently introduced charging, congestion remains a growing threat to efficiency and environmental quality. Surprisingly also, given the scale of digital tech locally, the roll-out of ultra-fast broadband has been very slow – Bristol lies 54th out of 63 towns and cities in 2022 – and this is another potential brake on efficiency and investment.

Bristol has clearly performed well in economic terms and delivered in terms of prosperity and lifestyle for many of its communities. The underlying factors driving investment and growth remain. But as one of the country's most successful cities, it is now also one of the most expensive – both for housing, business and employment land. It has also failed, historically, to invest in efficient public transport which can, in turn, support higher density, less car-dependent, sustainable development. The threat is not immediate. The city has proved resilient in the short-term in the face of the Covid-19 pandemic, Brexit and recession, and many places across the UK would welcome the advantages which Bristol continues to enjoy. The danger, however, is of a gradual choking off of growth as more mobile households, more highly skilled workers, businesses and investors increasingly look elsewhere. ■

Martin Boddy is Emeritus Professor of Urban and Regional Studies at the University of the West of England (UWE Bristol) and a freelance consultant. He has a long history of researching and writing about UK cities including a particular focus on Bristol and the West of England.

"...Bristol has clear strengths from an economic perspective. But looking across different parts of the city it is clear that not all have benefited from economic success."

4.2

Bristol and Business: A Tale of Two Future Cities

Jaya Chakrabarti

I believe that business is a force for good.

We face many problems as a city: the Covid-19 pandemic and its impact, coping with Brexit, trying to mitigate climate change, delivering greater social justice. Business leaders have to think about the future of our organisations beyond our corporate structures and bottom lines. Even with the onset of AI, the majority of our workforce will still need breathable air, drinkable water, land on which to have stable, affordable housing, good education for children, and reliable, regular transport links. All businesses need to contribute to these and to making the lives of people in Bristol better.

In looking at the future of Bristol and business, I want to paint two pictures: the first pessimistic; the second hopeful.

Backwater Bristol 2033 is not a place you'd want to do more than visit for a weekend, or for work. It's aesthetically beautiful, but when you take off the green-tinted spectacles it's no greener than any other city. And it's unaffordable for the majority.

Most graduates wooed during their time in Bristol have found it too expensive to stay and many have returned home to save for their futures. Some good work has gone elsewhere as businesses have to rely more on international talent, a situation that many employers are familiar with thanks to our breaking of ties with the EU. Many in the tech sector are recruiting virtually. Others are adopting technology and replacing their human workforce with AI.

In the meantime, the lower-skilled jobs market has come to a standstill. Rents have risen, and with little affordable housing, affordable staff has become a distant memory. People are having to make a choice between food and heating. Companies in Backwater Bristol are having to adapt their business models significantly in order to produce goods and services that customers can afford. Our hospitality sector has had to evolve. With fewer front-of-house staff, the remaining small restaurants and pubs are making tough decisions. Downsized independent retailers, cafés and restaurants are seeing that only the largest in the sector are surviving through their scale and buying power to negotiate lower costs.

The business sector is having to pivot, downsize, offshore and/or restructure. Many have disengaged from wider community and city leadership. Moves to introduce living wages, paying suppliers on time, paying green business tariffs, conducting responsible sourcing, adopting ESG – environmental, social and governance measures – are all now deemed to be luxuries that will have to wait until the storms subside. If the paying customer cares, they'll pay lip-service, but no more.

With fewer people needing to travel to work in service businesses, buses only work on major routes. Public transport has never been fit for purpose but it's worse now, being either too expensive or not frequent enough to enable people to get to work around their family commitments. Good transport is not only essential for getting to places; it's important for social mobility, too, which has continued to decline.

In Backwater Bristol, schoolchildren are having to find other ways to get to school. Many primary schools had begun to close due to a lack of pupils back in 2023. In 2033, primary education in Bristol, as in the whole of the UK, is providing online access as the default option in certain areas. Parents have had to adjust their working hours in response and the isolation that was prevalent in pandemic lockdown days has rocketed. Mental health issues arising from this cannot be met by our healthcare services. With the pipeline of future employees affected by this shift, our city faces an uncertain future.

At this time, when Bristol needs leadership and a voice to speak for those who cannot, the opportunities with the 2024 shift to a committee system of city governance remain elusive. Decision-making is convoluted and unable to respond to crises. The appointed leader of the council is unable to negotiate without gaining consensus across all four parties and independents, leading to stagnation on much of the progress that had been made the decade before. The greatest loss is our voice and visibility nationally and internationally. In times of global instability, we have no one to speak for us and our values. Other city regions are louder, more united and more successful. Even Banksy has shifted his operations to (a far) Greater Manchester.

Backwater Bristol remains a collection of 34 villages held loosely together by a tarnished BS postcode and sticky tape. The relationship with our regional authority remains troubled, and while the other three West of England Combined Authority local authorities are able to speak with one voice, Bristol is an outsider to discussions and much of the dwindling funding available goes elsewhere. An unhappy electorate has just chosen once again to spin the referendum wheel to bring back a different governance model to fix what was broken....

That's a bleak view (and a deliberate provocation). There's a different future in Brilliant Bristol – another provocation.

There's no need for green-tinted spectacles in Brilliant Bristol 2033. We're lean and green and active. Why? Because businesses in the city made a choice to work with city leaders, enabling us to not only protect our most vulnerable but to see our institutions and businesses thrive.

Back in 2019, Mayor Marvin Rees set up the City Office and the One City Plan, creating a network and encouraging cross-sectoral working to address key issues faced by citizens. Even though a committee system was introduced in 2024 following the 2022 referendum, the future of the One City vision was secured by giving custodianship to the cross-party ceremonial mayor. City councillors now work hard with the network to ensure that the voice of the city on both the national and international stage is not lost with the change in governance. The city has moved from having one voice to many voices – but all singing in harmony. We've realised that it doesn't matter which form of governance Bristol has as long as we have a connected city.

This sense of civic identity, greater trust and involvement brings about city-wide and region-wide collaborations to safeguard the welfare of citizens. Businesses are working together with the city's public and third sectors to ensure that workers can afford to get to work on time while still being able to spend time with their families. Our responsibly used AIs are hooked up to our district heating networks. Nobody has to choose between food and heat. Subsided public-private bus routes are common. Libraries that could no longer be sustained in their original buildings have been distributed across numerous community and religious buildings. Trees line our streets, keeping them cool, and nature has taken root on our office building walls.

Affordable housing developments have grown above car parks and otherwise undeveloped land. Communities have come together to ensure that natural habitats are protected, and new nature corridors are emerging. The mutual aid networks that developed in the pandemic are now the foundation of community action groups tackling loneliness, mental health and vulnerability within their neighbourhoods. Our healthcare system is able to manage demand as our population is a much healthier one. Our people are living and dying well. A new connectedness is here, underpinned by thriving businesses made profitable by their local communities. The streets are safer thanks to our connected communities, and the idea of children walking and cycling to school no longer fills parents with fear. Our police are resourced and trusted. Our diverse communities are no longer isolated because employers are able to invest in them. Social mobility is improving, which is good for business and the lives of future generations.

The beauty of Brilliant Bristol is that because we've achieved all this here it can be achieved anywhere. Other city regions have already begun to notice.

What should the business sector do to help the city move forward? As well as 2023 marking the 650th anniversary of Bristol, it's the 200th birthday of Business West.

Over the past 35 years, the Bristol Initiative – a key part of Business West – has helped the city develop. Things have changed from 35 years ago and we need a new approach. The business sector provides work. But it also has an ongoing responsibility to create a better city and region and a fairer, more just and greener society.

An *affordable* city is one target. We need to contribute to affordable housing in areas with affordable public transport so employers can have an affordable, healthy workforce. We need affordable food, affordable heat, light, affordable (free at the point of delivery) healthcare, affordable sustainable transport, and reusable and sustainable products.

But we don't just want to stop at affordable. When we go beyond affordable into a state of thriving, we can help fix our bigger problems. All business *needs* to be a force for good if we're going to get there, and that's going to take leadership and integrity. We have leaders with integrity in Bristol. We just need them to believe that together we can make Brilliant Bristol a reality. ▧

Jaya Chakrabarti is a digital activist using open data and technology for good. She is the director of Nameless Media Group and the social enterprise Semantrica Ltd, which runs the corporate transparency platform TISCreport.org and eco-transparency platform projectvana.org. In 2021, she became the President of the Bristol Chamber of Commerce and Initiative.

Biography (from the future): Jaya Chakrabarti is a digital activist using open data and technology for good. She is the CEO of award-winning tiscreport.org which ended modern slavery in supply chains in 2030, and then achieved global afforestation with projectvana.org in 2032. In 2021 she became the first of many female, ethnic minority Presidents of the Bristol Chamber of Commerce and Initiative since 1823.

⌕ Imagine, either in words or pictures, your own Backwater and Brilliant Bristols. What change do you now want to make?

"There's no need for green-tinted spectacles in Brilliant Bristol 2033. We're lean and green and active."

4.3

Ghost Towns and High Streets

Jane Duffus

'**Do you remember the good old days** before the ghost town?'

That was the question posed by The Specials in 1981 in a song that brought to life the feeling of urban decay and deindustrialisation in Britain's inner cities. And this confirms that while the high street might look bleak today, it's looked bleak before and managed to bounce back. It's just a question of reinvention.

While rewatching an episode of the Bristol-based TV show *Shoestring* from 1980, I was struck by things in the background: the ease at which characters could drive and park in central Bristol, the plentiful presence of police officers, that all the shop units were filled by functioning businesses, and that many of those shops seemed to be independent concerns rather than chain retailers.

When I grew up in the 1980s and 1990s, the high street was the place to be. Cafés were packed, their windows misted with steam and cigarette smoke. A range of shops filled the units, with specialist and family-run businesses selling everything from vinyl records to snuff pouches. It was a treat to go shopping with your friends, have lunch and buy something new to wear that evening. The high street was a destination.

But walk around Broadmead, Bristol's shopping area, in 2023 and you see streets filled with empty shops, 'unit to let' boards pasted into windows and roads that are almost impossible to navigate. Car parks are prohibitively expensive, buses are running a skeleton service, public toilets have largely vanished, litter and graffiti prevail... Bristol gives every impression of being a city that actively wants to deter people from using its high streets.

Which of course is nonsense! The high street just needs to go back to its roots: community.

In the late Victorian era, the department store dominated. Thanks to the Industrial Revolution and the rise of people moving to more urban locations, community hubs were needed for people to carry out their errands... and the high street was born. At the most basic level, these new-found city dwellers no longer had the time or space to farm animals or grow crops, so they needed to buy groceries and other sundry goods. Market stalls expanded into shops and these retailers made a concerted effort with things such as customer service and home deliveries. Everything in the name of convenience. And what could be more convenient than a one-stop department store?

In London, for instance, Harrods (founded 1849) and Liberty (1875) were destinations, designed as places where women could escape the domestic sphere and spend a day unchaperoned. Selfridges followed the trend in 1909. This was still a time where a respectable woman was not seen out in public without a companion. Yet in a shop she was deemed safe, because she had a purpose and she had company.

The fortunes of the high street have bounced up and down ever since the recognisable concept of a shopping thoroughfare was established in the 1870s. And many of our high street staples date back to this era: Boots was founded in 1849, Sainsbury's in 1869, and Marks & Spencer in 1884, while WHSmith has been kicking around since 1792. The 1930s saw a boom for these chains because slack planning regulations meant they could buy up shabby old buildings, knock them down and construct uniform enterprises that fitted their aesthetic.

It's not all about commerce, either. The high street is a key location for political demonstration, too. If the bosses of a chain store have done something you don't agree with, why not litter their store with leaflets explaining the problem? If you've got a point to make, you can stand on a street corner and bellow it to anyone passing by. They might not take much notice, but you can't say you didn't try.

Suffragists and suffragettes used the high street to their advantage in the campaign for votes for women. As well as having grand shops selling branded merchandise, campaigners used the high street as a space for performance. Women took to the streets to sell copies of their newspapers. The Women's Social and Political Union (WSPU) launched a spate of arson attacks on property as a stand against taxation. In addition, militant suffragettes led campaigns of coordinated window smashing to get their message over that the government cared more about business than it did about women. This could go both ways, though. The WSPU shop on Queens Road in Bristol was trashed by male university students on 24 October 1913 as retaliation for the women burning down their sports pavilion the day before.

Obviously, the Great Depression and World War Two brought struggles for the high street, which didn't regain its stature until the 1960s when a new breed of customer demanded a new style of shopping (fun fashion, musical records, frivolous treats) and new types of stores to do it in. Mass production started to become the norm; self-service took over from customer service.

Bristol's shopping district was initially on Castle Street and Wine Street before both areas were decimated in the Blitz and a new shopping centre was constructed in the 1950s: Broadmead. This underwent further regeneration in 2010 following the opening of Cabot Circus nearby. But nothing could stop the domino effect of one store after another closing their doors for good.

Marks & Spencer vacated its large Broadmead store in January 2022 after 70 years, leaving an enormous void. Debenhams had already closed in May 2021. People no longer want the hassle of travelling to a city centre to shop with all the stress that this entails. These days, if people visit a real-life shop, it's because they want convenience. So they drive to an out-of-town mall where they can park easily, pop in and do everything under one roof. No hassle.

Even before the Covid-19 pandemic, the way people live and work was changing. Now, we largely shop online for almost everything. Many of us work from home, meaning we don't wander the shops in our lunchbreaks. Both office blocks and shop units are struggling to keep going. But none of this needs to signal the end of the high street because it can still provide a vital function for communities: the very thing that it evolved to do in the 1870s.

How do we create a future for the high street? It needs to offer something people can't get at home. And that means experiences. The high street needs to offer us food and drink, leisure opportunities, meeting places, medical services, beauty spas: things you can only get in person.

As such, there is an opportunity for independent traders to succeed where the big chains once dominated. Customers want to feel they are doing good: they want the feeling of community and want to know their cash is supporting a local trader, one who has made environmental decisions and has sound employment policies. People want to know where the food and materials they're buying have come from, and they want those items to be locally sourced. These are things small traders can provide but it's harder for a massive chain to give that reassurance.

People also want better air quality (ie from pedestrianised areas) and improved personal safety. The absence of the reassuring bobby-on-the-beat from Eddie Shoestring's day is lamentable. The signs on many shop doors saying dogs are now welcome is a great improvement. Accessibility also needs to be considered: people have a range of access needs that must be taken into account.

In 2011, retail guru Mary Portas was commissioned to write a report for the government about the future of high streets, for which one of her pilot areas was Bedminster. In hindsight, her project could be deemed unsuccessful: a number of shops in the area have since closed down, and West and East Street are still largely considered areas of deprivation. But change takes time. And in the years since 2011, East Street has gone from being solely occupied by greasy spoons and pawn shops to housing vegan cafés, an independent brewery, an artisan bakery... as well as seeing a rise in modern flats being built, attracting younger people. Is this a mark of failure or the slow realisation of what is happening everywhere? I'd argue for the latter.

Research from Deloitte shows that while the number of chain stores in the UK has decreased by six per cent since 2017, the number of independent stores has increased by three per cent. For instance, a former branch of Poundland in Catford has become a community space featuring food retailers, a cinema and café. In Bristol, the former Marks & Spencer store in Broadmead has become Sparks Bristol, a space where people can browse work by local artists, buy second-hand goods and explore what a greener future could look like.

But town planners need to re-energise the city to enable better public transport and easier routes across Bristol. I don't think it would be controversial to suggest that Bristol City Council has made some appalling planning choices over the decades and urgently needs to have a long hard look at ways to make Bristol a city to be proud of again. ▥

Jane Duffus has worked as a journalist and editor for numerous national magazines and publishers since 2000. She is a writer, editor and public speaker, and the author of six books including two in *The Women Who Built Bristol* series.

Q Learn about the Take Back the High Street campaign run by Power to Change. https://www.powertochange.org.uk/our-work/campaigns/take-back-the-high-street/

"The high street needs to offer us food and drink, leisure opportunities, meeting places, medical services, beauty spas: things you can only get in person."

4.4

Putting Work Futures in Their Place on a Bristol Industrial Estate

M Winter and Frederick Harry Pitts

The phrase 'future of work' likely elicits a mental picture punctuated by the presence of robots and the invisible authority of algorithmic management. It is no surprise that this sleek, high-tech vision of the future garners a range of emotional responses, from excitement to fear.

The excitement may come from an overly optimistic expectation of heightened efficiency, where organisations deploy a robot workforce devoid of human limitations or error. The positive implications of technological replacement are often anticipated most by those who will harness it to their benefit.

It is those workers who perform tasks that are apparently easily automated that are intuitively understood by the existing academic research on the topic as most fearful about this future of work. Coincidentally it is these workers who are often neglected in discussions about the future of work amongst academics, journalists and policymakers, who tend to foreground the stories and experiences of other graduates or professionals involved in digital roles in the knowledge economy.

Having cultivated a working environment associated with high-tech creative and digital industries, Bristol has been characterised by the Institute for the Future of Work as a 'Good Work Winner', with a higher-than-average provision of good work which 'builds resilience against social, economic and health shocks'. However, this comfortable accommodation to the changing world of work is far from a universal phenomenon. This highlights the need for approaches which allow for and recognise a more granular and contentious experience of transitions in working life. A place-based approach allows us to consider more closely the potential political consequences and challenges of everyday futures of work as they unfold in communities up and down the country.

It was this ethos that inspired our study of changes in working life on St Philip's Marsh Industrial Estate in Central Bristol. In January 2022, while employed at the University of Bristol, we began working together on a 'Bristol Model' project funded by Research England and the Office for Students, entitled 'Worker Perceptions of the Future of Work in Bristol'. We have since published a report, *The Bristol Project: Talking about work on a city-centre industrial estate*, on our findings with the Institute for the Future of Work.

St Philip's Marsh represented an interesting case study because of its status as a crucible for many of the shifts affecting the city. On the surface of things, Bristol does not fit neatly into the geographical, political, and cultural classification of the so-called 'left behind' spaces of industrial change commonly perceived as the target of the 'Levelling Up' agenda. However, pockets like St Philip's Marsh more closely resemble other areas of the country where shifts like industrial rebalancing, reshoring and the green transition present both risks and opportunities.

Moreover, its history is marked by change, transition and contested futures. In the mid-twentieth century, housing was demolished to make way for the industrial infrastructure of today. This consists of large warehouses for waste management, cement mixing companies, oil vendors and the like. Over the decades, many diverse visions of the future of the Marsh have been put forward and debated.

Having conducted more than 20 interviews with people who work and trade on the Marsh, we found that highly local prosaic and place-specific factors tangibly shape how workers view the future of their work and the firms or industries that employ them. The types of work performed on the Marsh are diverse. However, workers were aware of the place-based and material requirements of their work. For instance, one interviewee explained, 'You have to have somewhere in this area where people can work. And not everybody can sit and work in an office. Not everybody is good at that type of thing. You know, IT and selling insurance and banking and that type of thing. And you need hands-on people. You need somebody who can mend a lorry.'

Trading estates are an unsung but common part of the country's social, geographic and economic landscape – ecologies of industry and innovation that rarely get thought of as such. They are home to concentrations of small and medium-sized enterprises that play a vital role in the skilled trades, supply chains and services that underpin and power the local 'everyday economy', as well as regional industrial clusters. The type of work performed on St Philip's Marsh – being largely of a routine character – is often seen as most at risk to automation, an issue of vital concern to those interrogating futures of work.

It is undeniably true that technology plays a major role in shaping work. However, our foray into St Philip's Marsh revealed a far more complex spectrum of futures making themselves tangible to workers in the here and now. In fact, the relatively slow progress of technological replacement meant that it barely registered as a risk amongst workers there. Routine workers involved in the sorting of the city's recycling, the mixing of cement and the receipt of fruit and vegetable goods, for instance, face far greater uncertainty about their employment owing to proposed development plans than they do due to technology. Processes of local urban transformation, viewed as regeneration, often overlook the drastic and rapid impacts they can have on the lives of workers.

As well as being home to many routine jobs, industrial estates in many cities and towns have come to provide cheap, plentiful and adaptable space for entrepreneurs, creatives and artisan producers, as well as land ripe for acquisition by housebuilders and new mixed-use developments. These trends present a mixed picture for industrial estates.

On the one hand, we see the revitalisation of estates in line with new craft industries that in some cases, such as brewing, rediscover and reinvent trades that return to the foundation of these local industrial areas. These also contribute to new forms of employment that, despite superficial differences with many of the trades and professions associated with industrial estates, contain plenty of scope for shared issues and visions of good work.

On the other hand, regeneration can be bound up with perceived gentrification, even where planning initiatives seek to meet societal needs for housing for instance. Measures to bring about a greener environment, especially where a city-centre location means that the estate is seen as a source of pollution or other environmental concerns, can be a source of particular tension. These threaten to displace workers and businesses that have had little say in the matter and find themselves, their work and their industries at risk.

St Philip's Marsh exhibits many of these tendencies. Today, the area is subject to major transformation as part of the Temple Quarter regeneration plans. The 2021 report by Bristol City Council and partners, *Temple Quarter & St Philip's Marsh: A vision for the future*, explained that investment would 'unlock the potential to redevelop St Philip's Marsh creating new, sustainable neighbourhoods where housing sits alongside business and workspaces'. More specifically, St Philip's is imagined as a place for 'Creative and High Tech Innovation' nurturing a 'creative and knowledge-based economy of small and medium-sized businesses'.

Although plans for St Philip's Marsh are longer term, smaller and shorter-term shifts are already apparent, consistent with changes in other industrial estates across the UK. Established enterprises and industries are being augmented or replaced by new artisan and craft businesses like breweries, coffee roasteries, workshops for creative arts and event spaces. But, as St Philip's is set to go through yet another reimagining, it is vital to query whose vision is being implemented and whose vision may be being abandoned.

To do this we must focus our attention on a broader array of anxieties and tensions that occupy the space between the workplace and the wider 'place' within which work is grounded and granted its context. While residents may be consulted in changes and transitions where they live, workers are less often asked for their input on transformations affecting the places where they will likely spend much of their waking and working lives.

It is important to see work and workers constituting communities, and workers themselves as citizens within a set of civic relationships, to grant them voice over the changes that are afoot in cities and towns around green transitions, shifts in urban land use and other factors. This means that new channels and infrastructures of representation are needed to ensure the voices of working people are incorporated when developing futures of place which in turn have implications for futures of work.

Workers are subject to multiple, interacting shocks which transform conditions for work. These can drive adjustment costs for workers, which may be material or social. But workers do not always have clearly defined mechanisms to shape, contest or negotiate these changes. While greater worker voice at the level of the firm will inevitably be necessary to contest and coordinate the future of work as it is felt in the workplace, our work suggests it is equally important to ensure the needs of workers from across the economy are represented in broader processes of economic redevelopment and place-based transformation.

In Bristol as elsewhere, working people must be given as much a stake in the development of towns and cities as residents or business owners. It is only in doing so that planning initiatives and transition schemes can secure the full and broad local consent needed to be a success. ▧

M Winter is a post-doctoral researcher in the Department of Business Administration at Tallinn University of Technology in Estonia. She is also a research fellow at the Institute for the Future of Work in London, UK.

Frederick Harry Pitts is Senior Lecturer in Politics and Director of Business Engagement and Innovation in the Department of Humanities and Social Sciences at University of Exeter's Cornwall Campus. He is a Co-Investigator of the ESRC Centre for Sociodigital Futures.

Q Explore the plans for St Philip's Marsh
www.bristoltemplequarter.com/portfolio-items/st-philips-marsh/

5

CULTURE

What is the Future for Film in Bristol?

Robin Askew

At the height of the cinema boom, Bristol boasted 61 picture palaces. The advent of TV and subsequently video put paid to that golden age. By the 1980s, the showmen responsible for these often-ornate monuments to their egos were long gone, many of the fleapits had closed and the big cinemas were being carved up crudely into smaller screens.

Bristol somewhat belatedly got its first multiplex in September 1994. The Avonmeads Showcase was briefly the largest multiplex in the country, and also the most financially successful. The Showcase looks a bit careworn these days, but has inspired a certain amount of affection, as evidenced by the Showcase Avonmemes fan account on Twitter.

Other multiplexes followed. But while business boomed in the world of blockbusters, the main story in the years that followed – and continues to this day – is one of community fightback. The first battle came just a month after the opening of the Showcase, when loyal local cinemagoers swiftly gathered 1,500 signatures on a petition to keep the threatened Cannon Henleaze open. Their successful campaign saw an independent operator take it over and even restore the cinema's original name: the Orpheus. Today, it's run by the regional Scott Cinemas chain.

Next to go were the historic, family-run Gaiety in Knowle and the ABC Frogmore Street, which is currently the O2 Academy music venue. The well-heeled punters of Clifton were suitably appalled when the ABC Whiteladies Road was earmarked for closure in 1999. The historic ABC had actually thrived during the multiplex era, retaining its 5 per cent share of Bristol's cinemagoing market. A celebrity-supported Save the ABC campaign was launched, but the murky politics of property development meant that it remained boarded up until 2016, when it was finally reopened by the niche upmarket Everyman chain, who took care to restore much of its original marble grandeur.

If the commercial sector had been in trouble during the early eighties, the independents were hitting their stride. Boasting a cinema since the late 1970s, Arnolfini spearheaded regeneration of the city docks. Watershed media centre arrived in 1982 and went from strength to strength, adding a third screen and diversifying into VR technology.

The popular bijou, single-screen Arts Centre Cinema in King Square, which focussed mainly on repertory and second-run arthouse cinema, closed abruptly in 1998. But this too had a happy ending when the cinema was taken over by formerly nomadic avant-garde funsters Club Rombus who renamed it The Cube. It continues to thrive in its defiant independence.

More recently, and unexpectedly, Bristol's former IMAX cinema was brought back into use. Opened in 2000 as part of what was known as the Wildscreen At-Bristol project, this was the UK's third IMAX cinema. Alas, it lasted just seven years. Financial difficulties were cited when it was announced that the IMAX and accompanying Wildwalk exhibition were to close in April 2007 in order to save the more popular Explore attraction.

The IMAX cinema was then absorbed into the Bristol Aquarium. But in 2022, a bunch of enthusiasts sought to use the venue to screen films once again. The occasion was the first Forbidden Worlds cult film festival, which celebrated the 40th anniversary of that other great Bristol survivor: the 20th Century Flicks video rental store. This had itself been kept alive by installing two mini cinemas that are available for private hire.

Also recently brought back into occasional use by local enthusiasts, after negotiations with the current owner, is Totterdown's Old Picture House (originally the Knowle Picture House, which closed in 1961).

As we look to the future of exhibition, niche organisations are increasingly taking a key role, often making use of non-traditional screening spaces. Indeed, the Bristol Film Festival, founded in 2015, specialises in using such venues as Redcliffe Caves, Averys Wine Cellar, the Royal West of England Academy and the City Museum for its events. They've also screened *Airplane!* and *Top Gun* beneath the wings of Concorde at Aerospace Bristol.

In 2017, Bristol was designated one of 21 UNESCO Cities of Film. When the City of Film office announced its Summer Takeover of screenings in 2023, it was notable that not a single one of the nine free events took place in a traditional cinema.

In common with the rest of the arts, cinema took a big hit from the Covid-19 pandemic, which has proven to have a long tail. Watershed's long-serving Cinema Curator Mark Cosgrove reports that the cinema continues to operate at 25 per cent below pre-Covid levels of revenue. 'Everyone – certainly indie cinema-wise – is in a similar position,' he says. 'I'm viewing this figure – 75 per cent – as a new baseline and I remain to be convinced that it will go back to the glory days of pre-Covid.'

Prior to the pandemic, one of the main challenges facing conventional cinemas was the rise of streaming services. It seemed that great films financed by the streamers might never see the inside of a cinema in future. This situation was exacerbated during lockdown, but the streamers are now beginning to reach an accommodation with exhibitors. 'I do think that audiences spent Covid learning how to stream and valuing the home experience more,' argues Mark. 'Throw in cost of living and you have more challenges to get audiences to come to a venue and spend money. For a venue like Watershed, I think we need to focus on our difference/uniqueness – the kinds of films we show, the events and social side, and the curation (the personal touch rather than an algorithm).'

'Some streamers are recognising the importance of theatrical – in terms of raising profile/prestige and economically,' he adds. 'So Apple is giving Scorsese's new film a clear theatrical window. Interestingly, Netflix knows "there was money left on the table" with *Glass Onion*'s one-week theatrical, but their focus remains on subscriptions. Meanwhile, MUBI recognises the importance of theatrical and invests accordingly.'

Bristol didn't have any film festivals at all until 1982, when the biennial Wildscreen was inaugurated in the city that has become synonymous with the best in natural world filmmaking and now accounts for more than a third of all nature documentaries. Founded in 1995, the Encounters short film festival swiftly established an international reputation. Multiple niche festivals followed, including Afrika Eye, the Slapstick festival of classic and silent comedy, Cary Comes Home (celebrating Cary Grant), Bristol Radical Film Festival, Bristol Science Film Festival, Bristol Palestine Film Festival and the Cinema Rediscovered festival of restored archive gems, which now tours nationally.

In addition, Compass Presents stages popular 'expanded screenings' (i.e. screenings with performance elements) of such evergreen hits as *Monty Python and the Holy Grail* and David Lynch's *Lost Highway*. Other key local film groups include the Bristol Black Horror Club, Cables and Cameras, Bristol Bad Film Club, South West Silents and its offshoot Film Noir UK.

The local animation and natural history filmmaking sectors have thrived. But with a few rare exceptions, Bristol's rich potential as a filming location was poorly exploited until relatively recently. The innovative Bristol iFeatures initiative changed that with a trio of accomplished micro-budget feature films. 2012's *8 Minutes Idle* even became the first film to put Turbo Island on screen.

One of the most useful developments for filmmakers was the establishment of the Bristol Film Office 20 years ago. Its free service has brought countless film and TV productions to the city. Productions are also lured west by the state-of-the-art Bottle Yard Studios, the largest film and TV studio in the West of England, which recently opened its new TBY2 facility. This has proven a huge boost to the local economy. The Film Office's latest annual report revealed that film and TV production in Bristol generated £20.8 million in 2021/2022.

Nonetheless, there are many challenges ahead, which Bristol UNESCO City of Film Manager Natalie Moore identifies as: local skills shortages; limited funding for independent filmmakers; a London-centric industry and overly centralised sector support agencies; a disconnect between industry employers and new, diverse talent; barriers to employment and access to training; and heavy competition from other countries and UK regions.

'Many of these are reflected across the UK industry,' she observes, 'but there are ways in which Bristol is looking to address through new opportunities at a local level. One that I believe could have the biggest impact is the potential introduction of a regional production fund. Financial incentives are a major draw for feature films and TV drama productions. They also enable film offices to stipulate caveats in return; perhaps a percentage of locally based crew or new entrants from underrepresented backgrounds to be employed, or to ensure environmentally sustainable practices when working in the city. Regional policymakers are currently investigating a potential production fund and it could be a game-changer for growing the local production industry in a more inclusive and sustainable way.'

Brexit has had a significant impact in terms of access to funding and European talent ('Bristol's animation industry, for example, is facing heavy competition from European markets,' says Natalie) but it's the skills shortage identified by David Puttnam in a speech in April 2023 as the key challenge facing the British film industry that is having the greatest impact locally. 'There are major skills shortages across many production departments in Bristol and the wider city region,' Natalie adds. 'It's a national issue that is affecting all UK regions because of rapid industry growth and ever-increasing demand for new screen content. Skilled personnel are in high demand; often willing to travel and move between roles, putting pressure on production budgets as experienced workers demand higher wages and drive up recruitment costs. We're working to address this in Bristol, building a workforce development plan to support industry growth and ensure training and employment for underrepresented people. Bristol's film and TV industry will struggle to thrive without interventions that prioritise training and development of the workforce for the future. Enabling more localised industry access that builds a diverse, representative, and skilled industry crew base is fundamental to the future success of Bristol's film and TV industry.' ■

Robin Askew has spent nearly 40 years writing about film and music in Bristol. For more than three decades, he was Film Editor of local listings magazine *Venue*. He currently performs the same function for *Bristol 24/7* and is working on a long-gestating labour-of-love book project entitled *The West's Most Amazing Rock Shows 1963-1978*.

Q Discover cinema-going memories of people living in Bristol www.bristolideas.co.uk/projects/film-2021/ and learn about Bristol's film pioneer William Friese Greene www.bristolideas.co.uk/watch/peter-domankiewicz/

What Underground Culture Has Given Bristol

Melissa Chemam

After my book on Bristol's music and graffiti scene came out in March 2019, I spoke at the Bristol Transformed festival. I talked about how Bristol's colonial past came back around in the 1980s to build the culture that put the city on Britain's map, making its diversity a strength.

I had spent months interviewing key members of the scene: Robert Del Naja (also known as 3D, the first graffiti artist to make a name for himself outside the city, a rapper and member of The Wild Bunch and then Massive Attack), Inkie, Tricky, Ray Mighty, Neil Davidge, members of reggae bands Black Roots and Talisman, and Pop Group founder Mark Stewart, who sadly died in April 2023.

What I learned from our discussions and reflections is that without their 'Do It Yourself' attitude, none of them would ever have become artists. Not in the context of the late 1970s/early 1980s crisis and the rise of Thatcherism.

As the artists said, Bristol at the time felt deprived of cultural infrastructure compared to now. Then, young creatives could come to Arnolfini for free, to the Thekla for a small fee and to a few youth centres or pubs, but that was about all the public support they could get. And apart from Arnolfini and its 1985 'Graffiti Art' exhibition, few institutions showed interest in graffiti and hip-hop culture, which had emerged from underground. In fact, the local police did everything they could to destroy the graffiti scene and regulate house parties.

Luckily, the ethos of the reggae, post-punk and hip-hop cultures of that underground scene gave the strength to most of these young artists and wannabe musicians to carry on. No venue to perform at night? They made one happen: The Dug Out on Park Row, linking the areas of Clifton, Redland and St Pauls together. No space to hang out in the daytime? They used the Special K café and the Montpelier Hotel. They also met at record shops, squatted at the Glastonbury or Ashton Court festivals and expressed themselves at St Pauls Carnival.

But most of the 'Bristol Sound' and the graffiti art scene actually emerged in people's bedrooms, with 3D, Smith & Mighty, Mark Stewart, Miles Johnson, Tricky and Mushroom living 'on the dole', drawing stencils, writing lyrics or sampling tunes. Borrowing from reggae, dub, post-punk, hip-hop and soul, this music transcended these genres to create something new. It also offered a platform to some of the most incredible women's voices in Britain, from Shara Nelson to Beth Gibbons, Martina Topley-Bird and Liz Fraser.

Bristol culture radiates thanks to its diversity and inclusivity

Bristol contributed to the emergence of a new culture with this multicultural music. It came from immigrants from the former colonial empire. And it wasn't just Bristol. Outside the city, there were the likes of Neneh Cherry, Mad Professor, Sade, Keziah Jones, Skunk Anansie, Goldie, Lubaina Himid, Sonia Boyce and Keith Piper, and, in cinema, John Akomfrah, Isaac Julien and Steve McQueen.

A key strength of Bristol's underground scene was the transmission of immigrants' cultures: Caribbean fans of music, selectors of records for 'blues parties', pubs like the Bamboo Club, early DJs like Tarzan the High Priest and DJ Derek, who were doing the work from the late 1960s, long before it became a cultural trend, and probably many others whose names didn't make it into the news.

Bristol's colonial past, its links with the conquest of North America from as early as 1497 (when John Cabot's landing at Newfoundland in his voyage from Bristol gave England a territorial claim), wealth generated from the trade in enslaved people, and debates on whether to abolish slavery in now legendary pubs like the Seven Stars in Redcliffe – all these elements led to a long history of migrations, reinforced by two world wars and the displacement of the workforce known as the 'Windrush generation'. Their cultural influences touched the children of immigrants, those coming from the Caribbean and soon their Irish or Italian working-class neighbours in St Pauls, Barton Hill, Hotwells or Knowle West.

This outburst of uncontrolled and self-taught creativity led to cultural highlights which today are celebrated all over the world, from the multicultural sound of Massive Attack's third album, *Mezzanine*, to the three records of Portishead. From the graffiti scene came the meteoric rise of street artists like Inkie, Nick Walker and Banksy in the 2000s, all influenced by 3D and his precocious use of stencils.

Their success in the 1990s and 2000s changed the city.

When Banksy decided to come back to Bristol in 2009, he found a place to exhibit his work on a huge scale: Bristol Museum & Art Gallery – celebrating its 200th anniversary this year – saw over 350,000 admissions to the Banksy show that summer. An even bigger surprise came in the summer of 2015 when Banksy opened his own venue in nearby Weston-super-Mare – the ephemeral but successful Dismaland.

That same year, Bristol was the European Green Capital. Its streets were filled with inspiring cultural and nightlife venues; St Pauls was buzzing as much as the Harbourside. When my articles on Tricky's latest albums or Massive Attack's 2016 tour came out, everyone agreed with my observation that Bristol was one of the 'cultural capitals' of Europe.

Yet as early as summer 2019, I was also writing about the consequences of gentrification on neighbourhoods like St Pauls or Easton. Venues and pubs started closing. Petitions to 'Save the Nightlife' had emerged, led by Annie McGann and Leighton De Burca. Even Arnolfini had to stop exhibiting for a while, due to Arts Council England disinvestment, keeping their space on Narrow Quay open as a library and working space.

Later in 2019, I became the writer in residence at Arnolfini as they reopened with the 'Still I Rise' feminist exhibition. I wrote about the different cultures that were featured, once again highlighting the diversity of artists from Africa, the Caribbean, the Arab world and their diaspora.

A culture of resistance

'DIY' culture and diversity made Bristol the city I love so much.

Sadly, the lessons of these past three decades seem lost today. The current government is cutting funding for youth centres and arts degrees, and young creatives struggle to make a living, working on zero-hours contracts.

As artists struggle to get public funding, a lot of emphasis is put on technology, from virtual reality to artificial intelligence. It sometimes feels like public institutions have forgotten to invest in the beating heart of the arts: people.

I appreciate the efforts made by some to connect with more diverse audiences and improve their outreach. I also know of many who still feel unheard and unseen, as performers or as spectators. Each year, Bristol becomes more and more diverse, but many of its new communities feel underrepresented.

During the past few years, game-changing events have already shifted the future of Bristol: Brexit, the Covid-19 pandemic... But also the 2020 Black Lives Matter protests that led to the toppling of the statue of the slaver Edward Colston, who had been turned into a figure of so-called philanthropy.

The resilience of Bristol's cultural strength is also largely due to another phenomenon: its long history of activism. In terms of culture, Bristol would not be Bristol without the 1963 Bus Boycott, the 1980 St Pauls 'riots' and protests that followed, and the musicians supporting causes such as anti-racism, the anti-apartheid movement, Palestinian rights and justice for the victims of the 'Windrush scandal'.

In this, Bristol's world-renowned artists can be celebrated. Activists, too, such as the historian Roger Ball and the Radical History Group, and the former Lord Mayor Cleo Lake.

When Bristol's underground scene emerged, there were, despite the lack of funds or venues, many bands and hip-hop crews – not only The Wild Bunch, but Fresh 4, around

DJs Flynn and Krust, Smith & Mighty, FBI and later Roni Size & Reprazent. This allowed emulation, and inspired young people to believe it was possible to create new music.

Thirty years after the release of Massive Attack's first album, *Blue Lines*, which put Bristol on Britain's cultural map, some artists have shown that it was possible to do it again: the producers from the Young Echo collective, the singer-songwriter Laura Kidd (known first as She Makes War and now Penfriend), the post-post-punk band Idles, the internationally acclaimed Americana singer Yola. Others moved to Bristol for its underground scene, like members of the collective EP64, the DJ Batu, or the young non-binary singer-producer Tara Lily Klein, aka t l k.

It is important to foster a new generation, and it's crucial to not let anyone here believe they cannot exist because society shows them that they are bound to be underrepresented.

As the great photographer who documented the pioneers' journey, Andy Beese ('Beezer'), says: 'Create a scene to make a culture'. He also often quotes Mark Stewart, whose lyrics encouraged us to 'Kiss the future, protest and survive'.

To me, these words still sound like a mantra for the future of the city. ∎

Melissa Chemam is a journalist, broadcaster and writer on art, music, culture, social change, African affairs, North/South relations and activism. She is the author of the book *Out of the Comfort Zone* (Tangent Books, 2019), and currently writes for RFI English, Art UK, the New Arab, *Reader's Digest, UP Mag* and *Skin Deep*.

Q Read about Bristol's music scene and plan your next gig
https://visitbristol.co.uk/blog/read/2023/04/a-music-lovers-guide-to-bristol-b741

"The resilience of Bristol's cultural strength is largely due to its long history of activism."

5.3

Community, Not 5G: Beacons of Creativity Across Bristol

Emma Harvey

The BBC comedy-drama *The Outlaws* sees a group of misfits renovate Sea Mills Community Centre in north-west Bristol as part of a community payback scheme. In real life, the threat comes not from the construction of a 5G mast but from the local authority that is proposing to demolish the site – forced to close in 2019 due to structural defects – to make way for social housing.

In the show, community activist Myrna says, 'Developers, to get their plans approved, will promise you the moon on a stick and be gone in a week. But we'll still be here. We live here.' Though Myrna is fictional, the battle to save Sea Mills is real. Speaking to *Bristol Post*, a local resident said, 'The community has put in a lot of investment, time and energy into the building, and they don't want to see it go. The council will be up against an uphill struggle.'

The plight of this and other communal spaces isn't unique. In a bid to stave off administrators, Bristol City Council and other local authorities have been placed in the compromising position of repeated 'estates rationalisation' exercises to balance the books annually as costs of services outstrip budgets. Where they fail to do so, localities such as Croydon and Thurrock have been put into special measures. A campaign to save Thurrock Arts Centre is set against a backdrop of a £469 million budget black hole.

It's easy to pass by a closed or struggling community centre without giving it a thought when we're facing bigger problems like the demand for adult social care, a special educational needs crisis in schools, increased housing pressures and the ongoing challenge of climate change. But the state of community buildings, and the campaigns to save them, are the barometer of our societal health.

5G might connect us in the digital realm but it can't replace space, as character Myrna pleads, 'to go at night to study, to go to therapy, get rehab or learn to dance'. If the fix of our public finances is the continued depletion of publicly owned asset stocks, what happens when we've nothing left to flog? This policy, commonly dubbed 'selling off the family silver' after a 1985 analogy by former Tory prime minister Harold Macmillan, shows no sign of letting up 40 years on.

These beacons of creativity on our doorsteps are the beating heart of a city like Bristol. They are key to reducing our social care burden, educating our young people and connecting UK communities that are increasing in size and diversity. They contribute to economic security within their localities, pay taxes that help reduce national debt and provide us with somewhere to mobilise with others if we want to unite in response to the things that we care about. Historic England has even built the case for maintaining our historic social fabric not just because it is nice to have but because it is a vital part of the strategy to save our planet.

Council-owned buildings such as Windmill Hill City Farm, The Coach House (run by Black South West Network) and The Ardagh Centre demonstrate what is possible when local authorities entrust assets to the guardianship of ordinary folk. Bristol Community Land Trust and Knowle West Media Centre (KWMC)'s We Can Make homes show us what can be achieved when community groups take action in response to the UK housing crisis. The success of ambitious hyperlocal initiatives led by KWMC saw it shortlisted as one of ten organisations for the Calouste Gulbenkian Foundation's Civic Arts Award, celebrating its expertise in co-creation and building a sense of community identity and social cohesion.

The privately owned Tobacco Factory, generously leased over the next 999 years, is an example of the type of philanthropy that is rare in the UK and which could be more proactively cultivated and encouraged by political powers. Music venue The Exchange, arts centre Zion and Stokes Croft Land Trust have all shown how we can save much-loved cultural hubs through successful community shares models. Stephen Merchant, writer and star of *The Outlaws*, is backing a campaign in Redfield to save the old Wetherspoons and reinstate it as a community cinema.

To realise more of this, we need to move away from these projects being personal crusades, passion projects and the exceptional success stories, and towards a place where this is a proactively pursued model of regeneration that is embedded in long-term policy and strategy. There are a number of local and national funds, such as Youth Investment and Community Ownership led by Department for Digital, Culture, Media & Sport, as well as Bristol's £4 million Community Resilience capital scheme, which are targeted towards enabling communities to take on asset management. Capital grant schemes are notoriously difficult and often close without allocating all the funds that were made available. The successful Reaching Communities Buildings programme (2013-2017) led by the National Lottery supported 124 projects with £64 million, but this is 15 per cent lower than the target of £75 million funds and 150 projects.

Funding tied to political cycles and rigid conditions at best gives a few 'oven-ready' projects a brief moment to make good on their community's dreams. For others, the need to raise significant match funds or have a fully costed capital scheme that's ready to go and be completed is not a realisable prospect within a finite funding window. The dynamic between political and community stakeholders can sometimes act in a way that is counter to encouraging groups to prosper within their localities, with asset transfer conditions and processes both inconsistent and potentially counterproductive to success. The Community Interest Company (CIC) running Redcatch Community Garden, having transformed the site into a viable community hub, is now faced with the prospect of a rent increase of 2,000 per cent plus. Taxing revenues that could be used for local projects or to create jobs risks penalising successful groups for minimal gain and can feel like a scrabble for change down the back of the sofa when trying to pay your rent or mortgage.

Levels of investment such as the UK's annual arts sector spend is reflective of half of one month of the pandemic's Eat Out to Help Out scheme. Competitive fixed-term bidding processes force organisations to commit to overly ambitious programmes, unrealisable organisational development plans and subjective value measures like 'Dynamism' or lose out. Oldham Coliseum Theatre closed in March 2023, citing the decision by Arts Council England to drop it from its funding portfolio in spite of being in a 'levelling up' locality. There is often more to these decisions than is made public, but it seems strange that the people who stand to lose the most from a decision such as this don't get their say in these make-or-break decisions.

Escalating costs of multi-million, even billion, pound infrastructure projects, such as the doubling price of the Bristol Beacon refurbishment or HS2 construction, are seemingly justified with ease because of their projected economic value. Imagine what multiplying effect could be achieved if we adopted a similar mindset and distributed equitable support across communities and neighbourhoods.

In my lifetime, I long to see the city invest £100 million across every single change-making space in Bristol. With another £100 million, we could fund 100 new and emerging ideas and projects to create the KWMCs and Zions of tomorrow. The payoff of just a 50 per cent success rate would be a seismic shift in the way we think about and respond to the challenges facing us, giving us space to foster municipal support, increase our trust and understanding of one another and enable our homes to be built within a neighbourhood structure that connects instead of isolates. Spaces for lifewide democracy, for democracy from cradle to grave.

Funders and local authorities need to invest with their mindset, not just their money. Rather than communities swimming against each new political wave, Bristol has the opportunity to utilise the skills and assets network across the city to undertake a more proactive and bolder social and cultural infrastructure programme and, most importantly, to clearly define and protect a portfolio of assets that can serve as the foundation for future social strategy no matter who runs them.

Like Sea Mills, the Trinity Centre, where I'm based, is also publicly owned and we've run it on a full-repairing lease since 2003, transforming it from a liability into an asset of community value. Our lease expires in 2048 and I often play out what Bristol will look like by then. I'll be 68 years old, so it'd be amazing to think I'll be retired and dancing with neighbours and friends in my community hub. Failing that, you'll find me chained to Trinity's railings as I echo Myrna's 'Community! Not 5G!' war-cry: 'The real story is why aren't you news people camped outside the council offices asking the politicians why they're accepting money so they can knock down this community centre?'

I guess no one said retirement would be easy. ■

Emma Harvey is CEO of Trinity Community Arts, a charity formed to manage the Trinity Centre, a Grade II* listed building, community arts centre and independent live music venue. She has a background in the charity sector and in visual arts. She is interested in localism and developing inclusive spaces, platforms and technologies.

Q Could community-owned assets make a difference in your neighbourhood? Get advice about Community Ownership models www.communitylandtrusts.org.uk/

"These beacons of creativity on our doorsteps are the beating heart of a city like Bristol."

Why Bristol Needs Abolition Shed

Cleo Lake

In 1999 I was a gallery assistant for the landmark exhibition 'A Respectable Trade? Bristol and Transatlantic Slavery', the city's first real acknowledgment of its connections to the Transatlantic Traffic in Enslaved Africans (TTEA). Attendance was high and so were emotions. When the exhibition closed, a section of it moved to the Industrial Museum, which later became M Shed. The success of the exhibition was never really harnessed, especially in growing understanding and bridging fractured and divided opinion in the city.

Over 20 years later, the Edward Colston statue was toppled, a reparations and atonement motion was passed by Bristol City Council and the Bristol Legacy Group (BLG) commissioned the Project T.R.U.T.H. (Telling, Restoring, Understanding our Tapestry and History) consultation with African heritage communities. There have also been notable independent interventions, including the highly successful CARGO Classrooms, the Decolonising Memory memorial dance and app and an exhibition by Bristol Cathedral uncovering its memorials to enslavers. But there is still an obvious omission: a permanent, dedicated 'museum' to tell the story. Why nothing permanent of significance exists to date is likely indicative of the old power systems, deliberately or otherwise, that have kept their knee firmly on the neck of change for so long. But Bristol is now in a post-statue-topple reality. Change is possible, closer, more urgent. The world continues to watch and almost everyone is waiting for action. As support and inevitability builds, the question now turns to what form that might take and what its purpose will be.

Alongside longstanding reparations campaigns, the Black Lives Matter movement helped to globally expose the pain, trauma, Afriphobia and ongoing racism experienced by people of African heritage today. This reality needs more than just a laying out of historical facts. Any depiction of the past must be in the context of enabling the intersection of ideas and conscience, that can explain the present and offer a commitment to solve the future, particularly in the realm of racial justice and equity.

The report findings of Project T.R.U.T.H. provide a mandate for a 'dedicated facility that charts Afrikan history and its connection to the city'. Relabelled as a 'Story-House' rather than museum, making this dedicated facility a reality is now on the agenda of the BLG. Any telling of the story will be done in a sensitive way that can empower people of African descent. It will be a place to locate the narrative in pre-enslavement and pre-colonisation, acknowledging and respecting African contributions to global culture and civilization and charting resistance to enslavement and racism. Whilst presenting facts will be important, it cannot be a place of triggering trauma. It is also important that African heritage people are not only centred in the story but that they are centred in curating and telling the story.

The concept of the UnMuseum has been launched by Black South West Network. Initially a digital platform with the longer-term ambition of a physical space, UnMuseum is about valuing and creating alternative cultural collections and content with community-based archivists and cultural producers from minoritised communities.

Perhaps the most vocal of calls in recent years has come from the Abolition Shed Collective. Made up of former Countering Colston campaigners and others and led by historian Mark Steeds (co-author of *From Wulfstan to Colston*), the collective has been advocating for an Abolition Shed since 2016. Now renamed BEAMI (Bristol Enslavement and Abolition Museum Institute), the group proposes a facility that will tell an international story about enslavement and abolition. A focus would be on Bristolian women reformers such as Hannah More, contributions by working-class Bristolians, visits by African Americans including Frederick Douglass and the countless uprisings by the enslaved Africans themselves. An education facility for all, a core aim is to bring about a better understanding of Bristol's connection to this global shared history.

Story-House, UnMuseum, Abolition Shed are all possible. Maybe Bristol, in its new-found status as a decolonial epicentre, deserves to have and to offer all these possibilities, so that the goals of societal and systemic change, reparatory justice, racial justice, reconciliation and healing may be understood, accepted and permanent change achieved. ■

Cleo Lake is a community engagement professional, researcher and intuitive creative artist/producer. She was Lord Mayor of Bristol 2018-2019 and in 2021 was the lead consultant, researcher and report writer for Project T.R.U.T.H.

"Change is possible, closer, more urgent. The world continues to watch and almost everyone is waiting for action."

Bring Your Ideas
Caleb Parkin, City Poet 2020-2022

bring your ideas
and let's stitch them into the city, weave them through streets chattering with trees
and we'll sip your ideas, a little fizzy, a little bitter, with a slice of lemon or a pinch of salt

bring your ideas and serve them up
in a meal for 91 tongues, of cardamom, jerk seasoning, garam masala and cumin
serve them in the chalk horizons of equations, the antimatter of cosmic failure

bring your ideas and keep bringing them
even when they laugh, when you have to switch continents for a healing Yes
even if your ideas drop from towers into dark pools, fizzing with threat

bring your ideas and stencil them
on the wall of the tallest tower in the city, in a chart of the body's earth
we'll learn our edges in a quiet prayer for wellness, a hymnbook for health

your ideas might make us lightheaded or ease our pain
or can we drink them with marshmallows and whipped cream?
can we count them on one hand, eat them from a fruit-bowl?
or watch them in shoals and burrows, in fights for survival?

let's purple your ideas, infuse them with vitamin C
let them BUNGEEEEEEEEEEEEEEEE
maybe they'll smash in bright blue smithereens in the Gorge of Disappointment
or become smash hit tracks cut-up remixed and trip-hop glitched

bring your ideas and cast them
in bronze and pop them on a plinth and let's animate them
or cast them differently, turn them to clay then let them dance

let your ideas stop the bus until injustice gets off
let them magic lantern *Liberty* from Fishponds to the Docks
let's talk ideas across borders, over trenches
make them supersonic fledgelings

bring your ideas and let's live in them
together – share a bright green common, but keep a backyard
because sure, that new idea might become a regret
or a neighbour you wish you hadn't met
or maybe it'll be that BFF you haven't quite
nearly but – plucked up the courage to chat to – yet

6

FUTURE INFRA-STRUCTURE

The Future of Sustainable Food in Bristol

Louise Delmege

Food shortages have not been a problem for the UK since the Second World War.

Back then, we managed because the government stepped in and made sure we grew as much food as we could and bulk bought the rest from abroad. Since then it's been left to the supermarkets and we've comfortably settled into only producing about half of what we eat and importing the rest. Our supermarkets have developed an incredibly advanced system that allows us to have new, delicious and plentiful foods, whenever we want.

But disruption from trade deals agreed after Brexit and changes in consumer demand following the first Covid-19 pandemic lockdowns revealed how this system is balanced on a knife edge. There are no stores of food that could see us through disruption like this, and our vulnerable supply chains are getting more vulnerable as the government plans to import food from further and further away.

That's not to mention the increasing prices of food. Cheap food is often not good for our health but is important for our economy because cheap food means wages can stay low. But now, the cheap food that fuels a low-wage economy isn't cheap enough anymore, with people in work having to rely on foodbanks.

The UK food system is in a bad state. We should all be able to afford healthy food that's come through a supply chain where everyone involved can also comfortably afford it, and which is grown in ways that protect the environment, instead of destroying it.

Farmers are underpaid for their produce. The fees supermarkets are willing to pay them won't cover the increased costs resulting from climate change and increases in fuel and feed costs. This means they struggle to invest in new and more eco-friendly ways of working. Despite this, the food they produce still isn't cheap enough for low-wage workers to buy it.

This cost-of-living crisis isn't the only thing to worry about. Climate collapse is coming, and the solutions to these crises will not come from our politicians. Unlike during the war, our current government is unlikely to intervene in the economy to protect our food supply. Cross-party ideological opposition to economic planning – for example the Conservative-Lib Dem coalition government scrapping a 2030 national food strategy shortly after the 2010 election – means we've missed opportunities to make the changes we need.

This is where cities can come in. Within our city we can have a big impact, without waiting for national policy to change. In the face of future food insecurity, cities offer an opportunity to build sustainable food systems that could protect large numbers of people, and also have an impact far beyond their boundaries.

Rising to the challenge

In 2021, Bristol became the first of two UK cities to achieve Gold Sustainable Food City status, in recognition of the city's work to build a more sustainable, fairer and healthier food system that benefits people, communities and the planet.

And now, Bristol Food Network is working on a new plan to take this further – up to 2030. The Bristol Good Food 2030 Plan will set out what we can achieve as a city and steer us in the direction of a strong, more resilient food system.

In Bristol, businesses, charities and community groups collaborate with the council to make change through the 'One City Approach'. This makes it easier for organisations to influence the decisions that have the biggest impacts on citizens' daily lives. Following this approach, Bristol Food Network collates the priorities of businesses, public services and community organisations into one plan that we take to the council. We streamline the conversation, removing barriers and helping to find new ways forward when things seem too big to change. System change can't happen one issue at a time – we have to look at the whole system.

Because of the scale of cities, we can make tangible changes to our local environment and have an impact on the wider economy. Food businesses and groups can reduce plastic waste, lower local emissions with electric vehicles and buy more local and sustainable products. If we get the biggest businesses and public bodies to invest in local produce, that's a huge boost for local producers, and means they'll be able to grow more food closer to home.

Bristol is one of the most engaged food cities in the UK. Our Gold Award Submission showed the massive amount of work being done across the city by businesses, charities and individuals. Lasting connections have formed between organisations which now work as an interconnected web, collaborating on strategies and plans which we hope will make a tangible improvement to our city's environment.

Responding to a crisis

The response to the lockdowns showed how small community groups can step up.

More agile than larger service providers, small community organisations did fantastic work protecting vulnerable people during those critical months. A small group might not be able to slow global climate change, but they can protect their communities by building infrastructure that can be relied upon in emergencies.

Some of the most impressive lockdown support projects were led by a handful of people working tirelessly to redistribute surplus to people who needed it most. People who had never done anything like that before took on huge responsibility. Neighbours stepped up to help people they'd never met. Businesses used the furlough scheme to enable their workers to volunteer to cook and distribute food.

Jamaica Street Stores collaborated with the People's Republic of Stokes Croft to feed hearty meals to local citizens. Easton's Thali Café made thousands of halal chicken curries which were distributed by National Food Service Bristol for months. It was wonderful to witness how, when we have the time and the money to do so, people are overjoyed to give their energy to helping others.

Sadly, many of these organisations have since closed or reduced their services. The two largest food delivery projects active during the lockdowns, Matthew Tree and National Food Service Bristol, both stopped delivering shortly after the lockdowns ended.

A lot of the food funding which poured into charities also dried up, and what has returned since is not enough to cover rising costs. Frontline services are struggling with rising demands and rising costs.

Thankfully, there are a few exceptions to this trend. During the lockdowns, Heart of BS13 worked with Square Food Foundation, which reached out to furloughed chefs to prepare meals, which were delivered to families known to the charity. These are both long-running, locally rooted organisations aiming to make a big impact in a small area, rather than spread thinly. They know their communities inside and out. In a crisis, this information is essential.

Since then, Heart of BS13 has joined five other organisations as one of Bristol's first Community Climate Action Partners, meaning they've been granted thousands of pounds to invest in climate-conscious community development work. They'll be composting and growing produce for their local area, and teaching people how to grow, cook and eat their own healthy, environmentally friendly food.

Increasing what we grow within the city could present a vital resource in an insecure future and building strong links between groups so they can work together is insurance against the next disaster. Successful projects like this offer real hope in a difficult time.

A vision for a sustainable food city

Unfortunately, we're going to be in a much worse position the next time a crisis comes along. Voscur, Bristol's support agency for the voluntary sector, predicts we are going to see 'an utterly devastating reduction in services and projects available to communities in our city.' This will make us less prepared for the next disaster. We need good information sharing and collaborative working so we can quickly identify the areas in greatest need and support the people working there.

It's not an easy future for food, but Bristol is one of the best prepared places in the country to weather the coming storms. By investing in our community infrastructure now, we can protect vulnerable local people from the worst outcomes of climate change. Collaboration within cities presents the best opportunity we have to protect thousands of people.

The Bristol Good Food 2030 Plan sets out what we hope the city can achieve by the end of the decade, and our action plans describe what organisations across the city are already planning to do between now and the end of March 2024. This framework will forge more connections, helping make the most of available resources and working to have a positive impact on our food system.

If you want your organisation to make a difference in the city's food system, it doesn't matter how big or how small you are. You can bring your voice to essential conversations across the city. You can tell policy makers what your community needs to see change. It's the job of Bristol Food Network to help you get your voice heard.

Bristol Food Network's vision is to transform Bristol into a sustainable food city. And it's our role to support, inform and connect individuals, community projects, organisations and businesses who share this vision. ■

Louise Delmege is a partnership coordinator for Bristol Food Network CIC, working on the Bristol Good Food 2030 Plan. She brings together businesses, charities and the council to collaborate on improving Bristol's food system.

Q Join Bristol Food Network and get advice on growing, buying and sharing sustainable food https://www.bristolfoodnetwork.org/

"It's not an easy future for food, but Bristol is one of the best prepared places in the country to weather the coming storms."

Bristol Needs to Drive Less to Save the Planet. But This Only Works if We've Got a Viable Alternative

Matty Edwards

It was almost five years ago that Bristol rightly won plaudits for becoming the first council in the UK to declare a climate emergency and set the hugely ambitious target of reaching net zero carbon emissions by 2030.

But in 2023, with seven years to go, transport has been identified by the Bristol Advisory Committee on Climate Change (BACCC) as one of the areas where we're making the least progress as a city.

Not only is transport the biggest contributor in the region to emissions but, over the past 15 years, the data shows that almost no progress has been made locally on reducing carbon emissions from transport. In 2022, just over half of people in the West of England travelled to work by car. If we're to have any chance of reaching net zero by 2030, private car journeys will have to fall by 40 per cent.

But how to get Bristolians to drive less? Despite some investment in new cycle lanes, innovations such as the e-scooters and tackling pollution with the Clean Air Zone, Bristol still has to put up with failing bus services and patchy cycling infrastructure.

How to get people out of their cars?

Bristol City Council has used the Covid-19 pandemic as a springboard to place restrictions on driving, such as turning Bristol Bridge into a bus gate, pedestrianising the Old City and individual roads such as Cotham Hill and Princess Victoria Street in Clifton Village.

As the Clean Air Zone has shown, placing restrictions on cars – in this case charging people to drive the most polluting vehicles into the city centre – is controversial and risks causing uproar.

And now the council is embarking on the first of two liveable neighbourhood pilots to stop traffic driving through residential areas. First up is the East Bristol Liveable Neighbourhood in Barton Hill, Redfield and St George, which is being trialled this autumn before the scheme becomes permanent.

The large area of narrow residential streets is often used by cars cutting through to avoid the main roads. By stopping cars from doing this, the idea is that walking and cycling are encouraged while the neighbourhood becomes less polluted and nicer to live in.

The Bristol Cable has spoken to hundreds of local residents and investigated how other cities have tackled the issue.

Many residents support the liveable neighbourhood because they feel the area is currently dominated by cars squeezing down narrow streets, which can feel unsafe for pedestrians, and the council's early consultation showed general support for the scheme.

But now that the trial measures have been announced, there are also locals who think it will cause great inconveniences, especially those with mobility issues who can't easily walk or cycle. There are also concerns that it will push traffic onto surrounding main roads.

This concern is legitimate, but evidence shows it isn't always the case. A January 2023 study on the impact of 46 low-traffic neighbourhoods in London by the University of Westminster seemed to show they reduced traffic within their boundaries without always pushing it onto roads around their edges.

Another review, *Street Shift: The Future of Low-Traffic Neighbourhoods*, published by Centre for London in June 2022, found strong evidence that low-traffic neighbourhoods cut car journeys in and around the area and encourage people to use other transport. Although they may move some motor traffic to nearby roads in the short-term, this reduces over time.

The review found good design, engagement and communications can make low-traffic neighbourhoods more effective and less controversial. It said street improvements such as wider pavements, trees and greenery can increase low-traffic neighbourhoods' benefits, and that there must be support to help people switch to other transport. Early and comprehensive public engagement will improve public trust and schemes' quality.

Our reporting from the Italian city of Milan also showed that the key ingredient for success in their pedestrianisation of 38 squares and streets in residential areas was not just taking something away by restricting traffic and parking but offering something in the form of rejuvenated public space for people to enjoy, with benches, trees and colour.

This seems to have been grasped by Councillor Don Alexander, the cabinet member for transport, who spoke of the need for more consultation and how it's not just about cars.

'It's in many ways a public health intervention, not just even a traffic one,' he adds. 'We're talking about clean air, about kids being able to get to school using active travel, people chatting in the street and reducing social isolation.'

One Barton Hill resident we spoke to, Naz Nathoo, summed up how many others feel. He supports the liveable neighbourhood because his house has been driven into twice in the last three years as cars squeeze up his narrow street. But he said better public transport is needed if we're going to put restrictions on driving. 'To wait for a 36 [bus], you're waiting for God,' he said.

How to build public transport that is a genuine alternative

At the same time that Bristol is trying to get residents to drive less, bus services have gone from bad to worse with a driver shortage, temporary cancellations and routes being cut altogether earlier this year.

Bus services have been hit hard by plummeting passenger numbers during the pandemic, and had to be propped up by government funding.

The *Cable* spent months collecting hundreds of stories from bus passengers across the city. They told us about completely unreliable services making it impossible to get to work, timetables and live bus tracking being a complete fiction, and being forced to pay for taxis, walk home in the dark and drive more often.

The further deterioration of Bristol's bus services have added fuel to fire in the debate about franchising the region's services. A fully-fledged campaign is now calling for the services to be taken back under public control, which would mean private operators like First would have to bid for contracts to deliver services, giving the Metro Mayor more power to set routes, timetables and make sure less popular but important services still run.

The model that allows greater public control is common in Europe, exists in London and is now being explored in other regions of the UK, including Greater Manchester, Liverpool and West Yorkshire. But West of England Mayor Dan Norris is dragging his feet and hasn't yet committed to investigating the feasibility of franchising.

As we spoke to older residents living in Ashton Vale in South Bristol about being cut off after their local bus service was scrapped due to low demand, the need for franchising could not be clearer. These services may not be popular and therefore not profitable. But they provide a lifeline for a community who are now left with the option of getting a taxi or even moving to an area with better buses. Under franchising, it would be easier to subsidise these less profitable but important routes.

The West of England Combined Authority (WECA) has been awarded funding to explore public transport 'innovations', which has led to an £8 million scheme to give passengers free bus travel in the month of their birthday, WestLink, an on-demand bus service in Knowle, Totterdown and Windmill Hill, where passengers can order via an app, and WestLocal, a £2 million fund, enabling communities to set up their own transport schemes.

The birthday scheme was branded a 'gimmick', the WestLink demand service has been beset by technical problems and a local councillor in an area reeling from bus cuts said it was 'absolutely ridiculous' to expect local people to sort out an alternative themselves.

The reason money is being ploughed into these initiatives is that the funding from central government can't be spent on maintaining services. It feels obvious that how transport funding is set up must be reformed if we're to get people to change their habits so we can reduce carbon emissions.

The elephant in the room is the issue of mass transit. Reducing car journeys by encouraging walking and cycling and making bus services more reliable is important but can only go so far. A new transport system will be required if we're to get to net zero.

What this system will look like has been the subject of debate since Mayor Marvin Rees first announced his vision for a Bristol Underground in 2017. £15 million is currently being spent to explore how a light-rail metro network could be built with four lines, some of which would be built underground.

But the issue has become a politically divisive one. Rees' underground vision has come under fire from opposition councillors due to it being unrealistic and too expensive, and now Metro Mayor Dan Norris has joined the chorus of sceptical voices.

Bristol City Council and WECA are now squabbling over this likely cost from £4 billion to £18 billion. Last month Rees said his flagship project might not survive after his time in office comes to an end when Bristol City Council moves to a committee system next year.

According to the BACCC, a large well-funded public transport intervention is necessary to offer an alternative to the high dependency on private car use.

That much seems obvious. But first the issue of transit needs to become less of a political football so progress can be made fast. ■

Matty Edwards is the editor of community-owned local media *The Bristol Cable*. In 2023, he led a year-long solutions journalism project called The Future of Cities, looking at how to build cities fit for the future.

Q Read more about Bristol's Transport strategy. What do you agree with? Could you commit to making one less car journey per week?
www.bristol.gov.uk/council-and-mayor/policies-plans-and-strategies/bristol-transport-strategy

6.3

How People Power Delivers Community Energy Schemes

Sean Morrison

'People here are really energy conscious,' says Richard, who moved into his self-build eco-home with his wife and daughter last May. 'We've got the opportunity to be part of this kind of experiment and I feel pretty positive.'

He's referring to a microgrid that's being wired up to all 33 homes on his Lawrence Weston estate, on the northwestern edge of Bristol. It'll reduce his and his neighbours' reliance on the national grid, and at times the site will be completely energy self-sufficient.

On a sunny day, it's expected that most of the energy generated on the Water Lilies housing development will be drawn from the large solar panels on the houses' roofs. When there's not enough solar energy, a large Tesla battery will serve the local demand.

The homes and their solar panels will be connected to the battery system, which will be charged with any solar energy the residents don't use. Basically, if your neighbour is on holiday, the renewables their house generates won't go to waste.

Those behind the scheme reckon this technology, if rolled out at scale, could contribute to a vital shift towards green energy, necessary if the UK is to meet its net zero targets, which it's on track to miss.

The community grid will also save residents money on their bills, which, considering the soaring cost of energy we saw over the winter, was obviously music to residents' ears. Just how much they stand to save, though, isn't yet clear.

Only when the battery runs out will the site draw energy from the national grid. As all the houses are efficient, with Grade A energy performance ratings, the need for this will be minimal.

'A lot of the time, [the estate] will be almost like an 'energy island',' says Andy O'Brien, co-director of Bristol Energy Cooperative (BEC), a not-for-profit organisation that distributes funds raised from its energy projects in the local area.

BEC is funding the microgrid scheme, which does sound amazing: cheap, clean energy that's generated and consumed locally. But the problem is it only benefits the privileged few who can afford to fork out on and own an eco-home on the site, which is in one of Bristol's poorest areas.

Surely, to truly harness the power of community energy, it should benefit everyone? Confronted with this, O'Brien says the idea is that this microgrid system, if it works, will be a test bed for larger projects in the future that benefit the wider community.

But it's not like this technology is new – so what's the hold up?

In the late 1990s, the residents of a tiny Scottish island set out on a project that provided a model for sustainable community energy, using a similar system.

Completely cut off from the national grid, the Isle of Eigg relied largely on noisy and expensive diesel generators that ran for only a few hours a day. So the residents attempted to electrify the island, connecting everyone to an independent power grid that would provide them with clean, renewable energy around the clock.

The islanders formed their own energy company, and in 2008 they launched what was hailed as the world's first community 'microgrid' system powered by wind, water and solar. The project enabled them to halve their energy use and generate 90 per cent of their electricity from renewable sources.

So why can't we just scale up their Eigg model? The main issue, as always, is funding.

The Eigg project cost about £1.66 million and was largely funded by the European Union's Regional Development Fund. Without this, the scheme might not have been possible, and community groups looking to replicate or build on the model have to get creative.

In Bristol, the Water Lilies microgrid was funded largely by share offers from BEC members, which enabled the co-op to pay for the scheme's different elements, including the solar panels, networking and the Tesla battery.

'To have a serious impact, all this stuff only really works if you do it at scale,' admits O'Brien, adding that the UK is on track to fail to meet its 2030 net zero targets. 'In comparison to new-builds [like Water Lilies], retrofitting homes is much harder to do. But we need to do it, and that's why we and a number of partners across the city [are] looking at how to do that.'

But there needs to be a major attitude change toward renewable projects at national level, he says. '[Politicians] wheel this out to say that we still need fossil fuels, when it's just not true,' he says, pointing to new research showing that the government has given £20 billion more in support for fossil fuel producers than those of renewables since 2015.

'The sad thing is, it's not the technology that's the issue,' O'Brien says. 'There's so much we could do if we had a better system, where the money available was going to the right places – not fossil fuel companies.' O'Brien says, however, that at regional level there are opportunities in the pipeline.

In December 2022, Bristol City Council approved a two-decade project with City

Leap, a partnership between the local authority and American renewable energy company Ameresco Ltd, paving the way for hundreds of millions of pounds to be invested into the city's heat networks, retrofit and other renewable projects.

And elsewhere in Bristol – actually, it's only a stone throw away – there's another energy project that's making headlines: England's largest wind turbine, which is under construction in Avonmouth. Owned and managed by a community group, the revenue its energy production makes will be used to support the local area. Water Lilies residents will see it from their windows.

For the community, the wind turbine will be a financial asset, selling the energy it generates to the national grid. The turbine is expected to raise upwards of £100,000 a year for Lawrence Weston, revenue that will be spent supporting the area's residents worst hit by the energy crisis, on things like draught-proofing homes and boosting emergency funds.

The project was financed largely by Thrive Renewables, a renewable energy investment company, which provided £4 million. Other funders included Bristol City Council, the West of England Combined Authority and BEC, which supported the scheme with income from a solar farm project.

The ambitious scheme attracted attention not just because of its size, but also because those behind it were able to overcome notoriously tricky planning hurdles – requirements introduced by former prime minister David Cameron, which have made onshore wind farms a rarity – to get it off the ground.

Mark Pepper, who founded the community group, Ambition Lawrence Weston, told the *Guardian*: 'It is a massive achievement that we've managed to pull off as an impoverished community... I'm hoping it will give confidence to people that they can achieve things, confidence that they've got a better, brighter future and a stronger connection with the climate emergency.'

A big achievement, yes, but the financial benefits to the local community rely on the revenue made from selling energy to the national grid rather than powering the local area directly. So power isn't completely in their hands.

The people of Lawrence Weston will still stand to pay unpredictable costs to large energy companies. The community group that generates the energy still stands to be underpaid for their energy.

So, while these impressive Bristol schemes could make a small difference, there's still potential to be unlocked – potential that relies heavily on a change to the political system that makes it so difficult for these community-led projects.

But there was a glimmer of hope this year, when the House of Lords voted through amendments to the government's Energy Bill that campaigners say marked a momentous day in the world of community energy.

The amendments were based on a bill put forward by community energy campaigners Power for People, which they say would allow community energy schemes to sell their clean, renewable power to local people – and provide a guaranteed price for electricity. As of June 2023, the House of Commons had yet to vote on these amendments. ■

Sean Morrison is a reporter for *The Bristol Cable*, specialising in social issues and investigations.

Q Find out about community-owned energy projects, activity and advice in Bristol
https://bristolenergy.coop/

"...there's still potential to be unlocked – potential that relies heavily on a change to the political system that makes it so difficult for these community-led projects."

How Do We Build the Housing We Need in Bristol?

Paul Smith

I come to this essay about the future while also deeply immersed in the past dreams for housing in the city for work I have been doing on the history of the Hartcliffe estate. In 1943 the council's housing plan identified the need for around 30,000 new homes. Eighty years later, in 2023, the council's draft local plan identifies a need for around 30,000 new homes. I could conclude this article simply by saying that in 2103 the future city will have a need for 30,000 homes, which we could just summarise as *plus ça change, plus c'est la même chose* – the more it changes, the more it stays the same.

In seeking to meet its housing need, Bristol, like many cities, seems to be locked into a battle between the need for more homes, the need to protect the natural environment and the desire by some to see the historic skyline unchanged. New housing is often opposed not just in the backyard, but from anywhere within the eyeline. One person's developable brownfield site is someone else's clear view, urban park or conservation site. One person's developable scrubland is someone else's site of important biodiversity or crucial open space. All these things can be true – it is a matter of genuine dispute.

We need to go back to some core principles to understand the housing function of a city. Cities exist to bring people together – for work, for culture and leisure, to access health services and public services and for education. It's also where many people live; the UN estimates that two thirds of the world's population will live in cities by 2050.

The Universal Declaration of Human Rights (UDHR) includes a right to adequate housing. The starting point for social policy relating to housing should begin here. The UN states that this right 'Must provide more than four walls and a roof' and sets a list of factors which determine whether housing is adequate, including: security of tenure; access to services such as water, energy and sanitation; affordability; habitability, namely providing protection against the elements and being a safe place; accessibility meeting the needs of disadvantaged and marginalised groups; location providing access to health and social facilities and away from pollution or other hazards; and cultural adequacy, reflecting people's cultural identity. This is a significant list and one which we cannot say is met for all the citizens of Bristol.

As a start, the city, which is already committed to the UN Sustainable Development Goals, should also commit to Article 25 of the UDHR and the right to adequate housing. A plan should be developed for Bristol to meet these objectives, starting with an honest assessment of how far away we are from meeting each of the requirements of this part of Article 25. As part of this, Bristol needs to plan for a return to social housing accounting for more than a third of its housing stock (currently around 20 per cent), say by 2050.

We also need to ask what we mean by 'Bristol'. The city's boundaries have grown over time, incorporating surrounding villages. In 1373, when Bristol was granted its city status, it was little more than the central area of Redcliffe and Kingsdown. The most recent expansion in 1949 brought Bishopsworth, a village which predates the city, into Bristol. The original ambition after World War Two was a much more dramatic expansion, including Patchway, Filton, Hambrook, Mangotsfield, Kingswood, Downend, Warmley, Oldland, Whitchurch, Dundry, Long Ashton and Portishead, around twice the size of the current city. When the Centre for Cities publishes data about Bristol now, it combines the City of Bristol with South Gloucestershire.

Bristol, blocked from expanding in the 1940s, had to resolve its dramatic housing demand (the same housing demand as now) by building housing outside its boundaries for Bristol residents. Those developments included council housing in Keynsham, Cadbury Heath, Kingswood, Nailsea, Filton, Yate and Long Ashton. Bristol was able to expand its housing need by exporting them to those other areas. Bristol is now an island of council housing with municipal homes in the surrounding authorities all sold to housing associations.

My view, which will be both controversial and strongly opposed – possibly as strongly as the objections after the Second World War to the city's proposed expansion when the city leadership was compared to Nazism – is that Bristol can only meet its housing needs through a boundary expansion not dissimilar to the one the 'City Fathers and Mothers' envisaged in the 1940s, maybe even more extensive, taking in Keynsham too. This would give the city access to more land for new homes, a larger tax base and a boundary which reflects the reality of what constitutes the city if one looked at an aerial photo rather than the archaic local authority boundaries. Under such an expansion it would need to be reflected that there is a parish council structure in the areas currently outside the city, that should be replicated within Bristol, enhancing the identity and a certain level of autonomy of Bristol's historic villages and the twentieth-century housing estates.

There is a growing community-led housing sector within the city, giving local people more control over meeting their housing needs. Currently, the most successful of these has been Ambition Lawrence Weston. However, all are limited by the lack of financial capacity, leading also to the lack of human resources to drive forward their plans, which leaves them dependent upon the goodwill of housing associations to manage their projects or to operate only at a micro level. It should be remembered that Bristol's council housing stock includes around 60 high-rise blocks which are approximately 60 years old. There needs to be an acceptance that many of these (and other housing built in the 1950s and 1960s using factory methods) are beyond their useful life and are failing to provide good quality homes for their residents. For some the answer will be a major upgrade, as has been successful in Park Hill in Sheffield, but for most the future can only involve the wrecking ball and dynamite. It's not just about the individual blocks but also about the inhospitable neighbourhoods they have created with poor-quality open space and disconnected communities.

Who should decide which should be retained and which should be replaced? I would argue that this must be a choice of the residents. Bristol could tackle this – and some of the other issues of urban regeneration on council estates – by passing the estates into the ownership of the local community. Versions of this have been successful in other areas. Castle Vale, an estate in North Birmingham, was transferred to a community housing trust in the 1990s. In this model, the historic debt relating to the state was written off by the government and the trust received grant funding to assist with the costs of regeneration. In addition, as a housing association, the organisation can apply to Homes England for grants to build new homes. Another example is Poplar HARCA in Tower Hamlets, set up as a Housing and Regeneration Community Association. The association runs the housing and a range of other community services. Bristol would need to negotiate a financial deal with the government to ensure that similar organisations here would be able to manage significant regeneration funds, and the transfers would require a ballot of the tenants. In parts of the city, existing Community Development Trusts could take a lead in establishing these organisations; in others new organisations would need to be set up, or existing organisations could come together to create them.

One of the biggest challenges facing people in all types of homes – privately rented, social housing, owner-occupied – is their energy efficiency. Bristol has many homes which were built before the days of cavity walls. Currently, different schemes are available to different tenures of homes, leading to a piecemeal approach which is inefficient and expensive. Bristol could build on the concept of the City Leap – a partnership between Bristol City Council and Ameresco Ltd to accelerate green energy investment – to develop an area-based approach to decarbonisation and energy efficiency, mimicking the urban renewal schemes of the 1980s and 1990s. To achieve this, we will need a workforce skilled to undertake these huge and complex projects and the council will need to work with the sixth forms, colleges and universities to ensure that is possible.

People's homes sit at the centre of their lives. Unfortunately, many are failed by poorly designed or constructed homes and badly designed communities. Bristol has enormous talent, and using this to address the quality of our homes and neighbourhoods would have a significant impact upon many other areas of civic life, including health (physical and mental), care, cost of living, crime and anti-social behaviour, climate change and the local economy. The opportunities will require a partnership between the council, the government, public and private bodies and – importantly – the citizens of Bristol. The tenacity required would be great, the thinking long-term and the investment significant, but the benefits and returns would be enormous.

Paul Smith is CEO of Elim Housing, a charitable social landlord based in Bristol. He previously served as a Bristol City Councillor from 1988 to 1999, when he was Chair of the Environmental, Health, Land and Property and Leisure Services committees, and 2016 to 2020 when he was Cabinet Member for Homes and Communities.

Q Take a look at Castle Vale Community Housing in Birmingham https://www.cvch.org.uk/ and Poplar HARCA in East London. Could these models work in Bristol? https://www.poplarharca.co.uk/

"My view, which will be both controversial and strongly opposed... is that Bristol can only meet its housing needs through a boundary expansion..."

7

THE UNIVERSITY AND THE CITY

7.1

The Future University in the Future Bristol

Evelyn Welch

On 23 April 1908, the journal _Nature_ reported that the Treasurer of University College Bristol had received a grant from the Board of Agriculture to enable the department of economic biology to study the effect of electricity on plants and that the County Council of Somerset had approved 'a scheme of research in connection with Cheddar cheese-making'. It also noted that Gloucestershire County Council had resolved to support the movement for the establishment of a university in Bristol.

While the pledge of £100,000 by the Wills family to support the foundation of a new university is much better known, there were many donations and supporters and interested parties, large and small, that helped Bristol celebrate the receipt of its Royal Charter on 24 May 1909. The new University of Bristol was already a surprisingly large institution for the period, with almost 700 students, male and female. The quick accolade of several Nobel prizes for staff members, such as the mathematician Paul Dirac, cemented the university's high research reputation, but it continued to have deep local roots and a strong sense that the work done within the University's walls, whether on medicine or on the production of cheese and cider, should make a positive difference to its communities. This was not just for its Clifton campus staff and students. The Barton Hill settlement was set up around the same time, bringing the University to a community in a part of the city that was, and still is, very deprived.

In comparison to many of the UK's other greater universities, Bristol is a comparatively young institution. Our foundations remain at the heart of a new strategy for high-quality, broad-based education. Outstanding specialised research and civic engagement will take us forward to our 120th anniversary year and beyond. It has been a privilege to join the University at this time. I have been in post as Vice-Chancellor and President of the University of Bristol for just over a year, and every day I see the complex intersections of our history and our future. Our work in Barton Hill continues and we have advanced research departments leading globally significant discoveries in everything from robotics and environmental and life sciences to digital technologies, quantum, data science and population health. We collaborate with the other universities in our region, as well as with schools, NHS Trusts, charities and businesses based in Bristol and beyond. These collaborations have seen the development of, for example, new materials that will help Airbus make more sustainable airplanes, and ground-breaking projects like the Children of the 90s study, which has followed the lives of families in Bristol for over 30 years, leading to many important health discoveries.

Our students bring a diverse and dynamic population, enriching the cultural and social landscape which helps make the city so special. They bring huge benefits in terms of cross-funding regeneration of de-industrialised or de-retailed areas, breathing new life and vitality into parts of the city that need it. Added to this, more than 100 community and other organisations benefit from the support of thousands of student volunteer hours every year. Many of our students also choose to stay in Bristol once they graduate, creating a valuable, educated and growing workforce to help attract investment and create new opportunities for the region.

But there are challenges for our city and institution, too

The ability of all of the universities in our region to stay internationally competitive, and to continue supporting a more prosperous and dynamic local economy, is contingent on remaining financially resilient. We need to continue to grow but we also know that Bristol has become one of the most unaffordable UK cities to live in. According to the Office for National Statistics, more than 80 people a week relocate from London to Bristol and Bath, adding to a view that, alongside student number growth, Bristolians are being increasingly squeezed out. To address this, we have been working hard with the council to implement a plan of new purpose-built student accommodation to increase supply in parts of the city where student housing investment is beneficial to the local community, and to relieve pressure on other parts of the housing market. We are also exploring new approaches to integrate student housing with other housing needs, including, for example, via the development of new intergenerational housing.

Beyond the housing crisis, Bristol remains divided in terms of educational outcomes. Progression rates to higher education are particularly telling. In Clifton, one of the most affluent areas of the city, progression rates are 100 per cent. Conversely, in Hartcliffe, only eight per cent of learners are educated to university level. The divide is not simply north/south, however, with disproportionately low levels of progression in many areas of north-west Bristol, including Avonmouth and Lawrence Weston. I believe there is more the University can do to make a difference here.

More broadly, the University has a key civic role to play in several respects, particularly in terms of bringing our expertise to the fore. Bristol is big enough to have every kind of global problem you can imagine, but small enough that high-quality research can inform interventions – and it is possible to see the results of those interventions in near real time. This is unique, this is exciting and this is what we must do more of. We are fortunate to be based in a city that is willing to work with us to put our research into action.

Delivering on a plan for our shared future

Crucially, our strategy recognises that if we are truly going to help make a difference, we must do it collaboratively, inspired by our commitment to quality and excellence and in the way in which we work in partnership, within and outside the University. The commitment to being a global civic institution forms the third pillar in our strategy and is the most striking development from previous plans.

We are determined to open up the benefits of a Bristol education to more local students, with an ambitious target in the new University strategy of 15 per cent of all learners coming from the local area by 2025 (up from six per cent in 2021). Such a move will help to build on recent initiatives like the radical Bristol Scholars programme which guarantees all Bristol schools up to five places at the University for disadvantaged students. Through this initiative, the school assessment of student background and potential, rather than A-Level grades, are the dominant entry criteria.

Helping to provide a supportive environment for innovation in our region is another key civic priority. Throughout the last decade, we have engaged extensively with public and private sector partners to develop research and innovation themes, provide high-quality infrastructure, skills and finance, and identify local growth and regeneration opportunities. Fortunately, and not accidently, Bristol is already home to one of the UK's fastest-growing and most significant tech clusters. It boasts one of the highest business start-up and survival rates, enjoys globally recognised strengths in sectors such as aerospace, zero carbon and the creative industries, and is renowned for innovation in AI, 5G, semiconductors, quantum technology, cyber security, robotics, haptics and data science.

We aim to help our city region secure its future in these valuable sectors, and we relish the expectation and imperative that we will serve as a key innovation engine within the local area – a vital source of talent, skills, ideas, technologies, expertise and partnerships. Our developing Temple Quarter Enterprise Campus, central to the emerging Temple Quarter regeneration programme, provides just one example of this defining commitment.

Opening in 2026, the building has been designed from the ground up to support challenge-based research and education. The activities it will host will be co-created, co-developed and co-delivered with our partners. This will be a place to do things differently. We will inspire and equip our students with the skills to survive in a changing world. Alongside our academic researchers, social scientists, industrial technologists and entrepreneurs, they will work and partner with local businesses, global organisations and communities to solve real-world problems. From the future of work to the impact of cutting-edge technology on society, Temple Quarter will be a new destination for collaboration, innovation and opportunity that will benefit everyone. A new public realm will provide a hub for local communities, with open and welcoming spaces to socialise, shop and collaborate with others. In the evenings, at weekends and during university holidays, local people are invited to take part in lifelong learning programmes, social and cultural events, festivals and research activities.

This is an exciting moment. When I think of our strategy and our new campus in 2030, I think of how it might help a young person in Bristol, elsewhere in the UK or internationally. They are, perhaps, 11 or 12 years old today. They've only known a digitally enabled world (and are used to using technology to enhance their education in novel ways that create new opportunities). They have only known a world that has only really just woken up to the dangers of climate change. They have only known a world where the political, local and geopolitical have become more and more divided. We have a responsibility to make a place for them at our university and in our city, ensuring we help them create an equitable future for all. ■

Evelyn Welch became Vice-Chancellor and President of the University of Bristol in September 2022. She was previously Senior Vice-President for Service, People and Planning at King's College London, and had been Vice-President (Arts and Sciences) and Provost (Arts and Sciences). She has taught at University of Essex and the Warburg Institute and has held leadership roles at University of Sussex and Queen Mary, University of London.

> Q Discover the Civic University agreement, signed by both universities.
> How could you engage with this?
> https://www.bristol.ac.uk/university/civic-university-agreement/

"We are determined to open up the benefits of a Bristol education to more local students…"

7.2

Our City, Our Region, Our Universities – What Could the Future Hold?

Steve West

Our city region is an environment with huge diversity and opportunity. It has evolved and matured in its vibrancy as a cosmopolitan landscape spanning urban, rural and coastal geographies. Our economy is strong and innovative, and we have significant talent and creativity in our population.

But we have stubborn and substantial challenges to resolve. The question facing us as leaders is: do we have the courage and ambition to truly maximise our potential and work together to realise the best futures for the communities that we serve?

The inequalities we see in education and health outcomes, and experiences of economic and housing challenges, are unacceptable and morally unjust.

We are a city with huge opportunity and potential, juxtaposed with poverty and challenge, and this has to be solved if we are to become a leading player on the global stage.

How do we create this vision and plan to deliver a better future for all, working together as one city region?

I can start by setting out what UWE Bristol brings to the table.

UWE Bristol is in its 30th year as a university. But our roots stretch much further, beyond the days of Bristol Polytechnic and the Technical Colleges before this. Our heritage is founded on the education and skills needs of our region, working in partnership to create the highly skilled and knowledge-rich graduates that we need to contribute and lead across our city and beyond.

Over the last 30 years UWE Bristol has more than tripled in size, from 10,800 full-time students in 1992 to over 38,000 students and 3,800 staff in 2021-2022, becoming one of the largest providers of higher education in the South West. We have grown the opportunities for our communities and are powering our regional workforce, with over half of our graduates each year staying to shape our region, build sustainable and engaged communities, and boost the region's standing on a national and global stage.

At UWE Bristol we are hugely proud of our partnership ethos, working with schools, colleges, the public sector and industries to continue to strengthen the vibrancy and opportunity in Bristol and our region. Our partnerships have been long-term and sustainable and have delivered huge benefits.

For example, the UWE-led Future Quest regional partnership was set up in 2017 to combat the significant educational inequalities for young people in our region. Since then, we have worked with over 28,000 learners across 65 schools and colleges, significantly increasing progression rates to higher education and broadening awareness of career pathways and opportunities, complementing the important work we do with our partner schools through our School of Education.

We also recognise our key role in driving forward opportunity across the globe, showcasing what our fantastic region has to offer and helping boost skills and learning in parts of the world where we can bring significant benefit. At UWE Bristol we have seen our overseas provision increase ten-fold in the last ten years, providing transformational opportunities through 15 partner institutions in ten different countries. In 2021-2022 over 9,000 students were studying with the University overseas.

We are part of a global community, creating a future which embraces diversity of thought, celebrates creativity and drives forward innovation and improvement in our ways of living.

This is certainly the focus throughout our research – creating solutions to local and global challenges – across digital futures, health and wellbeing, creative industries and technologies, sustainability and climate change resilience. These are areas that will have huge impact for our communities and will empower our city region to showcase its contribution on the global stage.

It is also the focus throughout our business support and engagement. We play a pivotal role for businesses across the region, supporting 2,739 since 2018 to increase productivity, skills and academic expertise, creating a further 650 jobs, raising £9 million in private investment and seeing the creation of 300 new products.

I am hugely proud that UWE Bristol is in, of and for our city region and the West of England, creating inclusive opportunities and powering our economy through our wide-ranging economic impacts, our graduate-talent pipeline and support for innovation and enterprise.

But this is not enough. The future is challenging. We have to change the way we do things in our city region to thrive in the future and tackle the inequalities that are holding us back.

We are operating in a global knowledge and innovation economy that is moving incredibly fast. The environmental, political and technological advances we are seeing will require us to collaborate in ways we have not previously experienced, in order to maximise our creativity and solutions. How do we empower every individual who lives, works and studies here to realise their potential and play their full part in a global future?

We are in a strong position to have two great universities in Bristol, both contributing different opportunities in taught provision, research and innovation. We are complementary and have real potential to do more together. If we look to the wider region, we have four universities and four further education colleges all with quality education, skills development, research and enterprise that broadly complements rather than competes. We have a rich and diverse ecosystem and if we add in our school networks, we have an offer that supports every stage of development and life. Our recently signed Civic University Agreement takes us a step further on collaboration to benefit our local population.

But we are operating in a competitive environment. Many countries are investing much more in their college and university infrastructure, research and access to courses. There is a real danger the UK will slip behind and not be seen as a global leader in the future. This would have a massive impact on the UK's economy and the experiences and opportunities of every citizen.

So how do we maximise the benefits of our thriving regional landscape for individuals and our communities, and how do we push the boundaries of our current thinking? What would it mean if I could look to one place for information about the diversity of skills, learning and innovation provision in our region and what the different pathways might mean for me? What would it mean for the efficiencies we could create through our ecosystem and how we showcase our potential on the global stage, if we could take a much bolder approach?

As we look forward, I believe we need to radically rethink what universities are for, how they are funded and configured and how they contribute and work in partnership. Over 30 years ago, the Vice-Chancellor of the day, Alfred Morris, described a vision for UWE which was based on a 'Federated University' model. Over the years we have increasingly collaborated and brought into the university different types of colleges and provision. I now think we need to move from evolution to a more purposeful, accelerated change in the business model across our region. A model that allows us to better invest and differentiate our provision with specialisms that offer opportunity to all throughout their lives.

We are seeing huge advances in technology that are having an impact on every part of our lives and changing rapidly how we all work, socialise and learn. We need to build a vision for a new innovative group structure which brings together our great universities to better support investment, efficiency and productivity. Under one corporate structure we would have sub-brands and offers that meet different markets, societal and economic needs on a global scale.

I believe that to be able to remain globally competitive in research we must cluster our world-class research environments together and operate as one in the global race to deliver a science and technological superpower capable of solving global challenges. By working more effectively together we will strengthen inward investment, utilise our estates more efficiently and be able to increase our investment in our staff.

By more purposefully working in partnership, we will be able to connect better with communities and industry, better deliver and sustain our net zero commitments and maximise the use of technological advances including Artificial Intelligence and Machine Learning. On this journey, we would reduce cost and duplication in our ecosystem to invest more in our people, research, innovation, teaching and support for students, and to develop new career pathways.

UWE Bristol started its journey as a university in 1992, based on a vision for a new university focussing on the application of knowledge to the economic and social advantage of its region. We have stayed true to this throughout our 30 years. As we look to the future, we need to push the boundaries further. For me, the future is one of collaboration that supports differentiation and personalised learning – offering access and learning opportunities in multiple ways to meet different needs and empowering our city region to thrive. ■

Steve West is Vice-Chancellor, President and CEO of the University of the West of England, Bristol (UWE Bristol). He is the President of Universities UK (UUK) and Chair of the UUK Mental Health in Higher Education Working Group. He is Chair of the West of England Academic Health Science Network and Non-Executive Director for the Integrated Care Board for Bristol, North Somerset and South Gloucestershire. He is a Deputy Lieutenant for the County of Gloucestershire and was made Commander of the Order of the British Empire in 2017, for services to Higher Education.

🔍 Explore the five 'What if?' future scenarios proposed in the Future of Higher Education report published by EY in 2021
https://www.ey.com/en_gl/education/are-universities-of-the-past-still-the-future

---

"We are a city with huge opportunity and potential, juxtaposed with poverty and challenge…"

Concluding Thoughts

Naomi Miller

The Royal Charter of 1373 – 'The Great Charter of Liberties including erection into a County' – granted that 'Bristol be for ever in future alike separated and in all respects exempted from the said counties of Gloucester and Somerset both by land and by water, and that it be a county by itself'. The contemporary view of Bristol as a city with an independent streak seems to have been part of its DNA since these years.

In 1373, Bristol was the third largest city in England – before being overtaken hundreds of years later by the cities of the industrial revolution. But its desire to be bigger and better has not diminished. Bristol continues to see itself as a regional, national and global leader. How the city grows, and what it grows into, however, are fundamental questions to which we must always return.

The Charter also refers to liberties, freedom from outside jurisdiction and freedom to govern itself. What has this liberty meant to the people and institutions of the city – and to the people and institutions who came into contact with it? A number of essays in this collection discuss the importance of understanding our histories, both those known and those under-researched or covered up. Their authors have argued that acknowledging publicly the failures of the past is vital in knowing where the city is now and where it might go in the future. They believe that inclusive sustainable growth – growth that provides safe, liveable homes for all, opportunities for social mobility, and equitable access to healthcare and green spaces – is the only way for cities to flourish.

Bristol, like all places, is a work in progress. Many great things have been achieved – whether in architecture, aerospace, engineering, legal reform, civil rights, art, literature or film – but there is always more to be done. The extent of the crises that face us is often overwhelming and daunting. Our contributors have not shied away from this. They have portrayed difficult futures, stated hard facts and addressed the realism and the nuances of the challenges that Bristol and all cities will have to grapple with.

However, there has also been hope, pragmatism and, importantly, ideas. This book demonstrates that there is a wealth of visions and solutions in all parts of our civic and city life coming from institutions, individuals, companies and communities. In the past few years, Bristol has made a positive move forward with the huge City Leap investment to decarbonise the city. This, the work on the wind turbine in Lawrence Weston, the innovative We Can Make housing scheme in Knowle West and the community-led projects collaborating with Bristol Green Capital Partnership, among many others, are significant achievements and provide hope for the future.

These solutions need energy, collective action and, in some cases, policy changes, legislation and funding in order to be achieved. This is not work to be done alone but work that must be done together. Bristol can never be 'in future alike separated and in all respects exempted from' anywhere in the world, let alone our neighbouring counties as the 1373 Charter states. We are a key regional centre, an important global city, a port, a city of sanctuary in an ever-connected world.

If this book is rewritten in 2073 for Bristol 700, what might it say? What world will have been created? Will the issues here be things of the past, or ageing, deep-set sores?

The book has been a call to action to learn about the future of Bristol and encourage new ideas to come forward. I hope that you are now feeling energised, informed and ready to act. How will you play an active role in your city? How will Bristol's future citizens, our descendants, look back at us, the 650 generation? The idea of being a good ancestor focusses normally on people, on how we consider and prioritise the lives of future generations. Could a city be a good ancestor? How will future Bristol look back on Bristol today? With thanks and gratitude? With disdain and disbelief? The choice is ours to make. ▪

BRISTOL 650 OUR CITY. OUR HISTORY. OUR FUTURE.

Bristol 650 marks the anniversary of Bristol being granted its independence from other county authorities by King Edward III in 1373. This act made Bristol a county in its own right. Bristol 650 has been a year-long celebration of all things Bristol: who we are, where we come from, what we've done and where we're going. It's been a chance to tell untold histories, mark many city anniversaries and welcome new arrivals.

There were two main themes of the year:

We Are Bristol

We are a city of individuals, each with our own talents, skills, stories and opinions. We come together as a collective to make the city of Bristol – a city that is rebellious in spirit, collaborative, diverse and welcoming.

Where Do We Come From?

What is my story? Where do my family and I come from? What are the stories of and from my community? How does the history of my house and street fit into the wider city story? How has the city grown and evolved throughout history?

Throughout the year, there have been a variety of events and activities to celebrate Bristol and the people of the city: 650 singers raising their voices in Bristol Cathedral and St George's Bristol; 1373-style street art taking over shop windows; a trail of brightly coloured unicorns; a giant 650 hopscotch on College Green; objects from the city's museum collections being recreated in large-scale chocolate sculptures. There have been festivals, public lectures, walking tours, exhibitions and workshops. People of all ages have gathered together for shared conversations and memory sharing. There has been new conservation work and research into the collections at city institutions including Bristol Museum & Art Gallery and the Royal West of England Academy. Other important anniversaries have been recognised: community projects across the city honoured the legacy of the Bristol Bus Boycott; St George's Bristol concert hall and Bristol Museum & Art Gallery marked their 200th birthdays; Business West explored and collected its stories to mark two centuries of work.

It has been a project of the city, by the city.

Bristol 650 has been made possible with support from The National Lottery Heritage Fund and National Lottery players.

The Illustrator: Till Lukat

When I arrived in Bristol for the first time, it was a Friday evening in 2014. I had been hitchhiking and sleeping under the stars for three days, starting my journey in Berlin, Germany. It wasn't the first time I had travelled to the UK, but London had left me with the impression that people in England walked very fast and mostly wore suits. When you're travelling to a place by hitchhiking, you need a feeling of having arrived somewhere, because you've spent a lot of energy getting there. It wasn't hard to get that feeling in Bristol. The lively atmosphere of a Friday evening was just what I was looking for. I was happy to find that most Brits walk at a pretty average speed and that there are approximately the same number of people in suits as there are in Germany. I also learned that British people do drink tea all the time – although not out of tiny cups with one finger raised in the air like they did in my English class schoolbook, but rather from an enormous cup with some mysterious writing on it, saying: 'SPORTS DIRECT'.

Back then, in 2014, I was studying Illustration at the University of Arts in Berlin, and my trip to Bristol left such a strong impression that I decided to do my Erasmus at UWE Bristol on its Illustration course. I loved UWE's campus, directly next to the deer park, and, right before going back to Germany, I met my girlfriend there. After university, she moved to Berlin and stayed there for five years until we decided to both move back to Bristol. Today we are married and I'm visiting UWE again, but this time as a guest lecturer in the Illustration department (the same course we met on). How is that for a full circle? I have fallen in love with Bristol in more than one way, and that's the feeling I wanted to capture for the cover art of the Bristol 650 book.

I came up with the idea for this illustration while taking a stroll through Bristol Harbour, a place where the present and the past are very close to each other. Fancy coffee shops with cappuccino-sipping freelancers line up beside a historical Fairbairn steam crane from 1878. In my illustration, this idea is taken into the future. What lies ahead of us in Bristol's historical harbourside? Hopefully some more greenery. Is the harbour in use again, but with solar-powered ships? Maybe the free space will be used for vegetable growing. Whatever it is, the seagulls will still be there.

Till Lukat is an illustrator and comic artist. Originally from Berlin, Germany, he has been living in Bristol for three years.

Bristol 650 Zine:
A Guidebook to Creating Future Bristol

An online zine has been created alongside the book, and you can read the two publications together or separately. Use the QR code to visit the zine.

The zine offers a guidebook for making change – in Bristol and wherever you are – happen. We can all make positive change in this world. Have a play and click on the illustrations and icons – many will lead you to articles, films, websites and organisations.

This zine is also an invitation to dream your future Bristol. It is designed to help you explore the radical histories of the city, the people who have helped to create social and environmental change and the landmarks of Bristol's protest culture. Happy exploring.

The Bristol 650 zine was designed by **Grace Kress**, who produces design, illustration and community engagement projects to strengthen social justice actions. She sees art as a powerful tool that brings communities together, makes information accessible and inspires positive change. She is the founder of Shelby x Studios, an online zine-making platform that centres C.A.R.E.: community, art, rest and education. Collaborating with artists and campaign groups, her creative practice aims to imagine the world without systems of oppression, making futures of freedom and joy our reality now – one zine at a time.

Acknowledgements

We have many people to thank in getting this book into print.

This publication is made possible with support from The National Lottery Heritage Fund and National Lottery players.

The board of Bristol Ideas, especially Suzanne Rolt, Simon Cook and Sheila Healy, have supported Bristol 650 throughout and we are grateful for this as well as support for general Bristol Ideas work.

We are grateful to all the contributors for their work, to Till Lukat for the cover illustration, to Grace Kress for the accompanying zine and to Bristol Books for publishing the book. Thank you to our four City Poets, Miles Chambers, Vanessa Kisuule, Caleb Parkin and Kat Lyons, for allowing their poems, written during their time as City Poets, to be included here. Andrew Kelly would like to thank the people he interviewed for his essay.

Our volunteers, Molly Websdell and Julia Stafford, and Darren Bane, from Bristol Books, helped greatly with the many drafts of this book. We'd also like to thank Clive Burlton, Joe Burt and Richard Jones for working on the publication and for advice throughout.